Introduction to Great Books

SECOND 2 SERIES

The Great Books Foundation
A nonprofit educational corporation

ISBN 0-945159-98-6

15 14 13 12 11 10 9

Published and distributed by

The Great Books Foundation
A Nonprofit Educational Corporation
35 East Wacker Drive, Suite 2300
Chicago, Illinois 60601-2298

Formerly published as Junior Great Books Series Eleven

Acknowledgments

All possible care has been taken to trace ownership and secure permission for each selection in this series. The Great Books Foundation wishes to thank the following authors, publishers, and representatives for permission to reprint copyright material:

Barn Burning from COLLECTED STORIES OF WILLIAM FAULKNER. Copyright 1939 and renewed 1967 by Estelle Faulkner and Jill Faulkner Summers. Reprinted by permission of Random House, Inc.

In Exile from ANTON CHEKHOV: SELECTED STORIES, translated by Ann Dunnigan. Copyright © 1960 by Ann Dunnigan. Reprinted by arrangement with The New American Library, Inc., New York, N.Y.

Equality from CONCEPTS AND CATEGORIES by Isaiah Berlin. Copyright © 1956 by the Aristotelian Society. Reprinted by permission of Viking Penguin, Inc.

Sorrow-Acre from WINTER'S TALES by Isak Dinesen. Copyright 1942 by Random House, Inc. and renewed 1970 by Johan Philip Thomas Ingerslev. Reprinted by permission of Random House, Inc.

Why the Americans Are Often So Restless in the Midst of Their Prosperity from DEMOCRACY IN AMERICA by Alexis de Tocqueville, edited by J. P. Mayer and Max Lerner, a new translation by George Lawrence. Copyright © 1966 in the English translation by Harper & Row, Publishers, Inc. Reprinted by permission of the publisher.

After the Ball, translated by Lesley Chamberlain, from THE PENGUIN BOOK OF RUSSIAN SHORT STORIES, edited by D. J. Richards. Copyright © 1981 by Lesley Chamberlain. By permission of Lesley Chamberlain.

Habit from PSYCHOLOGY: BRIEFER COURSE by William James. Copyright © 1962 by The Crowell-Collier Publishing Company. By permission of Macmillan Publishing Co., Inc.

The Overcoat from DIARY OF A MADMAN AND OTHER STORIES by Nikolai Gogol, translated by Andrew MacAndrew. Copyright © 1960 by Andrew MacAndrew. Reprinted by arrangement with The New American Library, Inc., New York, N.Y.

Contents

I

Shared Inquiry

A Great Books discussion explores the meaning of a selection that everyone in the group has read in advance. Discussion begins with a leader's interpretive question—a question about a problem of meaning that interests her in the selection. After reading the selection carefully, she has no answer to her question or she thinks that her question can be answered in more than one way. In either case, she wants to explore it with the group. Because leaders and group members work together to try to resolve such problems of meaning, we call the method of discussion *shared inquiry.*

As you discuss the problem, the leader will ask questions for several purposes: to help you clarify your remarks or support your answers with evidence from the selection, to make sure everyone will be given a chance to offer opinions, and to keep discussion moving toward a resolution of the problem.

As a group member, you need not wait to be called on. You may speak up at any time. You may respond directly to other group members as well as to the leader. You may express agreement or disagreement with what others say, add your own thoughts, or ask questions related to the problem being discussed. If you are called on but have nothing to say at the moment, you are equally free not to answer. If you have an idea that you are unsure of, or if you don't know whether your idea is a good one, don't be afraid to express it anyway—it may prove more valuable than you think.

To encourage group members to think for themselves and to guarantee that no one is excluded from discussion, shared inquiry has four rules:

1. **No one may take part in the discussion without first reading the selection.** If you have not read the selection, you cannot contribute to the discussion because you are unprepared to offer opinions and to support them with evidence from the selection.
2. **Discuss only the selection that everyone has read.** If you refer to other essays or stories, the participants who have not read them will be denied a chance to contribute to the discussion. This rule also enables the group to check the validity of what is said by referring to the assigned selection.
3. **Do not introduce outside opinions unless you can back them up with evidence from the selection.** If you get an idea about the meaning of a selection from an outside source—for example, the opinion of someone you know or an insight from another book—you may use the idea in discussion only if you can express it in your own words and support it with evidence from the selection.
4. **Leaders may only ask questions—they may not answer them.** If leaders stated their own opinions about the meaning of a selection, you might feel less inclined to think for yourself. You might also be less likely to believe that other equally good answers were possible. As a participant you are not limited to offering answers; you may ask questions, too. ■

By and About Aristotle

(384–322 B.C.)

Aristotle said that philosophy grew out of wonder:

> It is owing to their wonder that men both now begin and first began to philosophize. They wondered originally at the obvious difficulties, then advanced little by little and stated difficulties about the greater matters, e.g., about the phenomena of the moon and those of the sun and of the stars, and about the genesis of the universe. And a man who is puzzled and wonders thinks himself ignorant (whence even the lover of myth is in a sense a lover of Wisdom, for the myth is composed of wonders); therefore since they philosophized in order to escape from ignorance, evidently they were pursuing science in order to know, and not for any utilitarian end.

His own curiosity ranged wide. He wrote on the importance of experience in scientific investigation:

> Lack of experience diminishes our power of taking a comprehensive view of the admitted facts. Hence those who dwell in intimate association with nature and its phenomena grow more and more able to formulate, as the foundations of their theories, principles such as to admit of a wider and coherent development, while those whom devotion to abstract discussions has rendered unobservant of the facts are too ready to dogmatize on the basis of a few observations.

On the policy of tyrants:

> Their first end and aim is to break the spirit of their subjects; they know that a poor-spirited man will never plot against anybody. Their second aim is to breed mutual distrust. Tyranny is never overthrown until men begin to trust one another, and this is the reason why tyrants are always at outs with the good. They feel that good men are doubly dangerous to their authority—dangerous, first, in thinking it shame to be governed as if they were slaves; dangerous, again, in their spirit of mutual and general loyalty and in their refusal to betray one another or anyone else. The third and last aim of tyrants is to make their subjects incapable of action.

> Nobody attempts the impossible. Nobody, therefore, will attempt the overthrow of a tyranny when all are incapable of action.

On age and youth:

> Elderly men . . . have lived many years; they have often been taken in and often made mistakes; and life on the whole is a bad business. The result is that they are sure about nothing and under-do everything. They "think," but they never "know"; and because of their hesitation they always add a "possibly" or a "perhaps," putting everything this way and nothing positively. They are cynical; that is, they tend to put the worse construction on everything. Further, their experience makes them distrustful and therefore suspicious of evil. Consequently they neither love warmly nor hate bitterly, but . . . love as though they will some day hate and hate as though they will some day love.
>
> Young men . . . would always rather do noble deeds than useful ones. Their lives are regulated more by moral feeling than by reasoning, and whereas reasoning leads us to choose what is useful, moral goodness leads us to choose what is noble. They are fonder of their friends, intimates, and companions than older men are because they like spending their days in the company of others and have not yet come to value either their friends or anything else by their usefulness to themselves. All their mistakes are in the direction of doing things excessively and vehemently. . . . They think they know everything, and are always quite sure about it; this in fact, is why they overdo everything. . . . They are fond of fun and therefore witty, wit being well-bred insolence.

Aristotle's search for the ideal state and the best constitution is at the heart of his Politics. *Politics, for Aristotle, meant the scientific study of the polis, or city-state, and the art of governing it. The city-state he knew was a small, intimate society whose members were closely related to one another by ties of kinship, custom, law, duty, and affection. In our selection, Aristotle considers how the state began and what purpose it serves. Because he thinks that the best way to understand a thing clearly is to consider its origins, he first looks at the simpler social groups out of which the state grew: the union of man and woman, the family, and the village.*

Politics

Aristotle

Every state is a community of some kind, and every community is established with a view to some good; for mankind always act in order to obtain that which they think good. But, if all communities aim at some good, the state or political community, which is the highest of all, and which embraces all the rest, aims at good in a greater degree than any other, and at the highest good.

Some people think that the qualifications of a statesman, king, householder, and master are the same, and that they differ, not in kind, but only in the number of their subjects. For example, the ruler over a few is called a master; over more, the manager of a household; over a still larger number, a statesman or king, as if there were no difference between a great household and a small state. The distinction which is made between the king and the statesman is as follows: When the government is personal, the ruler is a king; when, according

---

*A selection from *Politics*.

to the rules of the political science, the citizens rule and are ruled in turn, then he is called a statesman.

But all this is a mistake; for governments differ in kind, as will be evident to any one who considers the matter according to the method which has hitherto guided us. As in other departments of science, so in politics, the compound should always be resolved into the simple elements or least parts of the whole. We must therefore look at the elements of which the state is composed, in order that we may see in what the different kinds of rule differ from one another, and whether any scientific result can be attained about each one of them.

He who thus considers things in their first growth and origin, whether a state or anything else, will obtain the clearest view of them. In the first place there must be a union of those who cannot exist without each other; namely, of male and female, that the race may continue (and this is a union which is formed, not of deliberate purpose, but because, in common with other animals and with plants, mankind have a natural desire to leave behind them an image of themselves). . . .

. . . When several families are united, and the association aims at something more than the supply of daily needs, the first society to be formed is the village. And the most natural form of the village appears to be that of a colony from the family, composed of the children and grandchildren, who are said to be "suckled with the same milk." And this is the reason why Hellenic states were originally governed by kings; because the Hellenes were under royal rule before they came together, as the barbarians still are. Every family is ruled by the eldest, and therefore in the colonies of the family the kingly form of government prevailed because they were of the same blood. As Homer says:

> Each one gives law to his children and to his wives.

For they lived dispersedly, as was the manner in ancient times. Wherefore men say that the Gods have a king, because they themselves either are or were in ancient times under the rule of a king. For they imagine, not only the forms of the Gods, but their ways of life to be like their own.

When several villages were united in a single complete community, large enough to be nearly or quite self-sufficing, the state comes into existence, originating in the bare needs of life, and continuing in existence for the sake of a good life. And therefore, if the earlier forms of society are natural, so is the state, for it is the end of them, and the nature of a thing is its end. For what each thing is when fully developed, we call its nature, whether we are speaking of a man, a horse, or a family. Besides, the final cause and end of a thing is the best, and to be self-sufficing is the end and the best.

Hence it is evident that the state is a creation of nature, and that man is by nature a political animal. And he who by nature and not by mere accident is without a state, is either a bad man or above humanity; he is like the

> Tribeless, lawless, hearthless one,

whom Homer denounces—the natural outcast is forthwith a lover of war; he may be compared to an isolated piece at draughts.*

Now, that man is more of a political animal than bees or any other gregarious animals is evident. Nature, as we often say, makes nothing in vain, and man is the only animal whom she has endowed with the gift of speech. And whereas mere voice is but an indication of pleasure or pain, and is therefore found in other animals (for their nature attains to the perception of

* *draughts.* Checkers.

gregarious
Tending to form a group with others of the same kind as a herd | pack | flock

• Appropriate to the purpose at hand
- A means to an end

 Inexpedient - inadvisable

pleasure and pain and the intimation of them to one another, and no further), the power of speech is intended to set forth the expedient and inexpedient, and therefore likewise the just and the unjust. And it is a characteristic of man that he alone has any sense of good and evil, of just and unjust, and the like, and the association of living beings who have this sense makes a family and a state.

Further, the state is by nature clearly prior to the family and to the individual, since the whole is of necessity prior to the part; for example, if the whole body be destroyed, there will be no foot or hand, except in an equivocal sense, as we might speak of a stone hand; for when destroyed the hand will be no better than that. But things are defined by their working and power; and we ought not to say that they are the same when they no longer have their proper quality, but only that they have the same name. The proof that the state is a creation of nature and prior to the individual is that the individual, when isolated, is not self-sufficing; and therefore he is like a part in relation to the whole. But he who is unable to live in society, or who has no need because he is sufficient for himself, must be either a beast or a god: he is no part of a state. A social instinct is implanted in all men by nature, and yet he who first founded the state was the greatest of benefactors. For man, when perfected, is the best of animals, but, when separated from law and justice, he is the worst of all; since armed injustice is the more dangerous, and he is equipped at birth with arms, meant to be used by intelligence and virtue, which he may use for the worst ends. Wherefore, if he have not virtue, he is the most unholy and the most savage of animals, and the most full of lust and gluttony. But justice is the bond of men in states, for the administration of justice, which is the determination of what is just, is the principle of order in political society.

Interpretive Questions

1. If the state is "prior" to the individual, is it therefore more important?
2. If the state is a natural development, why did someone have to found it?
3. Why does Aristotle think self-sufficiency is desirable for the state but not for an individual?
4. Why is a person who by nature lives without a state a lover of war?
5. Does Aristotle think the family is more important than the individual?

By nature, all men have a social instinct + when isolated he is not self sufficient - therefore he is like a part in relation to the whole.

II

Greek historian – 5th century B.C.
author of "History of the
Peloponnesian War"

Great Writers

Reading what Thucydides has to say about the relationship between great powers and their satellites, or what Thomas Hobbes has to say about human nature and government, or what John Dewey has to say about the formation of habits can change the way we look at things. We may not agree with these writers, but as we come to understand what they say, it is unlikely that we will ever again think about foreign policy or government or habit in quite the same way.

This kind of writing is rare. The depth of thought it conveys often makes it difficult to understand. We need to work hard to make a great writer's ideas our own. For making an idea our own is not a simple matter of agreement or memorization. It means becoming so familiar with someone else's thought that we can turn it around, consider it from different angles, and then decide how it fits with our own ideas.

Great writers give us the opportunity to form our own opinions on the basis of the most profound thinking that has ever been expressed. They require us to think about what it means to live in the world and about what we are and what we hope to become. As we make an effort to understand great writers, we find ourselves seeing further, as Isaac Newton put it, "by standing upon the shoulders of giants." ■

By and About Thomas Hobbes

(1588–1679)

In his autobiography Thomas Hobbes calls fear his twin, but his claims to be a timid man reveal more wit than truth. Although he favored obedience to authority, Hobbes developed a political philosophy that antagonized everyone who held power during his lifetime. Before his death he was barred from publishing anything concerned with human conduct.

Hobbes was also interested in the science of his day. After meeting Galileo in Paris, he was more alive than ever to the idea of motion, by means of which he accounts for perception and imagination:

> For after an object is removed, or the eye shut, we still retain an image of the thing seen, though more obscure than when we see it. And this is it the Latins call *imagination,* from the image made in seeing. . . . Imagination, therefore, is nothing but *decaying sense,* and is found in men and many other living creatures, as well sleeping as waking. . . . This *decaying sense,* when we would express the thing itself, we call *imagination,* as I said before. But when we would express the *decay,* and signify that the sense is fading, old, and past, it is called *memory.* So that imagination and memory are but one thing, which for diverse considerations hath diverse names.

According to Hobbes, we come to understand others by means of self-examination:

> Whosoever looketh into himself and considereth what he doth when he does think, opine, reason, hope, fear, etc., and upon what grounds; he shall thereby read and know what are the thoughts and passions of all other men upon the like occasions. I say the similitude of passions, which are the same in all men—desire, fear, hope, etc.—not the similitude of the objects of the passions, which are the things desired, feared, hoped, etc.: for these the individual constitution and particular education do so vary, and they are so easy to be kept from our knowledge, that the characters

> of man's heart, blotted and confounded as they are with dissembling, lying, counterfeiting, and erroneous doctrines, are legible only to him that searcheth hearts.

Discovering the truth requires language:

> For truth and false are attributes of speech, not of things. And where speech is not, there is neither truth nor falsehood. Error there may be, as when we expect that which shall not be, or suspect what has not been; but in neither case can a man be charged with untruth.
>
> Seeing then that truth consisteth in the right ordering of names in our affirmations, a man that seeketh precise truth had need to remember what every name he uses stands for, and to place it accordingly; or else he will find himself entangled in words, as a bird in lime twigs; the more he struggles, the more belimed.

Happiness, he said, "consisteth not in the repose of a mind satisfied." Instead,

> felicity is a continual progress of the desire from one object to another, the attaining of the former being still but the way to the latter. The cause whereof is that the object of man's desire is not to enjoy once only, and for one instant of time, but to assure forever the way of his future desire. And therefore the voluntary actions and inclinations of all men tend not only to the procuring, but also to the assuring of a contented life, and differ only in the way.

Hobbes was a great wit, and it is said that in the last years of his life he amused himself with epitaphs prepared by friends. His favorite was "This is the true philosopher's stone."

Hobbes held that the cause of the civil wars that plagued England during his lifetime lay in human nature itself. In Leviathan, *he proposes a solution to the problem of social turmoil: He argues that human beings will live in harmony only when the laws of society are enforced by an awesomely powerful government—a "leviathan," or monster, that can inspire terror in its citizens. Without such a government, discord is inevitable, society will collapse, and individuals will find themselves back in the lawless "state of nature," where life is "solitary, poor, nasty, brutish, and short." In our selection, Hobbes explains why governments must have absolute power to ensure peace and security.*

Of Commonwealth

Thomas Hobbes

It is true that certain living creatures, as bees and ants, live sociably one with another (which are therefore by Aristotle numbered amongst political creatures) and yet have no other direction than their particular judgments and appetites; nor speech, whereby one of them can signify to another what he thinks expedient for the common benefit: and therefore some man may perhaps desire to know why mankind cannot do the same. To which I answer:

First, that men are continually in competition for honor and dignity, which these creatures are not; and consequently amongst men there ariseth on that ground envy and hatred, and finally war, but amongst these not so.

Secondly, that amongst these creatures the common good differeth not from the private; and being by nature inclined to their private, they procure thereby the common benefit. But man, whose joy consisteth in comparing himself with other men, can relish nothing but what is eminent.

*A selection from *Leviathan*.

Thirdly, that these creatures, having not (as man) the use of reason, do not see, nor think they see, any fault in the administration of their common business; whereas amongst men there are very many that think themselves wiser, and able to govern the public better, than the rest: and these strive to reform and innovate, one this way, another that way, and thereby bring it into distraction* and civil war.

Fourthly, that these creatures, though they have some use of voice in making known to one another their desires and other affections; yet they want that art of words by which some men can represent to others that which is good in the likeness of evil and evil in the likeness of good, and augment or diminish the apparent greatness of good and evil, discontenting men and troubling their peace at their pleasure.

Fifthly, irrational creatures cannot distinguish between *injury* and *damage,*† and therefore as long as they be at ease they are not offended with their fellows; whereas man is then most troublesome when he is most at ease: for then it is that he loves to show his wisdom and control the actions of them that govern the commonwealth.

Lastly, the agreement of these creatures is natural; that of men is by covenant only, which is artificial: and therefore it is no wonder if there be somewhat else required, besides covenant, to make their agreement constant and lasting, which is a common power to keep them in awe and to direct their actions to the common benefit.

The only way to erect such a common power as may be able to defend them from the invasion of foreigners and the injuries

---

* *distraction.* Forcible division; drawing apart.

† *injury and damage.* By injury, Hobbes means intentionally hurtful speech or words. By damage he means actual loss of property or bodily harm.

of one another, and thereby to secure them in such sort as that, by their own industry and by the fruits of the earth, they may nourish themselves and live contentedly, is to confer all their power and strength upon one man, or upon one assembly of men, that may reduce all their wills, by plurality of voices, unto one will: which is as much as to say, to appoint one man, or assembly of men, to bear their person; and every one to own and acknowledge himself to be author of whatsoever he that so beareth their person shall act or cause to be acted in those things which concern the common peace and safety; and therein to submit their wills, every one to his will, and their judgments, to his judgment. This is more than consent or concord; it is a real unity of them all, in one and the same person, made by covenant of every man with every man, in such manner as if every man should say to every man: *I authorize and give up my right of governing myself to this man, or to this assembly of men, on this condition, that thou give up thy right to him and authorize all his actions in like manner.* This done, the multitude so united in one person is called a COMMONWEALTH, in Latin CIVITAS. This is the generation of that great LEVIATHAN, or rather (to speak more reverently) of that *mortal god* to which we owe under the *immortal God* our peace and defense. For by this authority, given him by every particular man in the commonwealth, he hath the use of so much power and strength conferred on him, that by terror thereof he is enabled to perform the wills of them all, to peace at home and mutual aid against their enemies abroad. And in him consisteth the essence of the commonwealth; which, to define it, is *one person, of whose acts a great multitude, by mutual covenants one with another, have made themselves every one the author, to the end he may use the strength and means of them all, as he shall think expedient, for their peace and common defense.*

And he that carrieth this person is called SOVEREIGN, and

said to have *sovereign power;* and every one besides, his SUBJECT.

The attaining to this sovereign power is by two ways. One, by natural force; as when a man maketh his children to submit themselves and their children to his government, as being able to destroy them if they refuse; or by war subdueth his enemies to his will, giving them their lives on that condition. The other is when men agree amongst themselves to submit to some man, or assembly of men, voluntarily, on confidence to be protected by him against all others. This latter may be called a political commonwealth, or commonwealth by *institution;* and the former, a commonwealth by *acquisition.*

Political commonwealth - Commonweath by acquisition
when men agree to submit
to one man.
man makes his children submit to his government
or by war

Interpretive Questions

1. Why must a sovereign chosen by the people use terror to perform the people's will?
2. Why do the members of the commonwealth make their covenant with one another rather than with the sovereign?
3. Does Hobbes think that fear is the only reason for obeying the sovereign?
4. Would change be likely in Hobbes' commonwealth?
5. Why must each member of the commonwealth "acknowledge himself to be the author" of whatever the sovereign does for the common peace and safety?

III

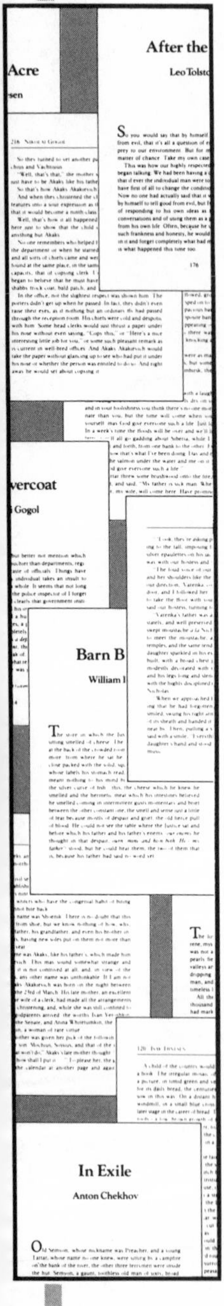

What a Story Is

A famous writer once claimed that a novel should "hold a mirror up to the high road," catching and reflecting the passing scene just as it occurs. But even the most realistic fiction does something more interesting than this. Although a story may tell us a great deal about life at a given time and place, it is before all else a personal interpretation of experience. Thoughtful writers do not merely copy or imitate life, they shape it and endow it with meaning. As we read a story, we experience the world ordered by a particular intelligence and filtered through a particular sensibility. We see through the author's eyes. If we lend ourselves to the story fully, if we are seriously attentive, open, and alert, it may forever alter our own vision.

The best stories generally balance conflicting claims or points of view. As in life, situations in fiction are complex. Characters who are at odds with one another may both be right—or more likely, there will be right and wrong on both sides. Thoughtful stories present characters in the round, showing us more than we would know if we were in the story ourselves and more than we usually understand about the lives of those around us. By thinking about such stories, we come to see how each person has a distinct point of view—his or her own needs, desires, sorrows, and reasons for acting. We learn to look, in a conflict of interests, for the whole picture. Reading fiction not only broadens our sympathies for others but challenges us to re-examine ourselves, to move beyond our usual habits of perception and judgment.

Good stories require us to reach out to the author through active reading. As we read, it's important to ask ourselves what the author is trying to convey. What does he want us to think and feel? Why is he telling us this story? How does he feel about these characters? Does one character perhaps speak for the author?

Ultimately, readers must rely on their own responses to a story. A story then becomes a joint creation of the reader and the writer, a joint effort to make sense of life: a shared world created through words, to be imagined, explored, and interpreted. ■

By and About William Faulkner

(1897–1962)

Faulkner on his goal as a writer:

> My ambition is to put everything into one sentence—not only the present but the whole past on which it depends and which keeps overtaking the present, second by second.

On his creative process:

> With me, a story usually begins with a single idea or memory or mental picture. The writing of the story is simply a matter of working up to that moment, to explain why it happened or what caused it to follow.

On the genesis of his novel, *The Sound and the Fury:*

> It began with a mental picture. I didn't realize at the time it was symbolical. The picture was of the muddy seat of a little girl's drawers in a pear tree where she could see through a window where her grandmother's funeral was taking place and report what was happening to her brothers on the ground below. By the time I explained who they were and what they were doing and how her pants got muddy, I realized it would be impossible to get all of it into a short story and that it would have to be a book. And then I realized the symbolism of the soiled pants, and that image was replaced by the one of the fatherless and motherless girl climbing down the rainpipe to escape from the only home she had, where she had never been offered love or affection or understanding. I had already begun to tell it through the eyes of the idiot child since I felt that it would be more effective as told by someone capable only of knowing what happened, but not why.

On the source of his material for writing:

> I'm inclined to think that my material, the South, is not very important to me. I just happen to know it, and don't have time in one life to learn another one and write at the same time. Though the one I know is probably as good as another, life is a phenomenon but not a novelty, the same frantic steeplechase toward nothing everywhere and man stinks the same stink no matter where in time.

On art:

The aim of every artist is to arrest motion, which is life, by artificial means and hold it fixed so that one hundred years later when a stranger looks at it, it moves again since it is life. Since man is mortal, the only immortality possible for him is to leave something behind him that is immortal since it will always move. This is the artist's way of scribbling "Kilroy was here" on the wall of the final and irrevocable oblivion through which he must someday pass.

Barn Burning

William Faulkner

The store in which the Justice of the Peace's court was sitting smelled of cheese. The boy, crouched on his nail keg at the back of the crowded room, knew he smelled cheese, and more: from where he sat he could see the ranked shelves close-packed with the solid, squat, dynamic shapes of tin cans whose labels his stomach read, not from the lettering which meant nothing to his mind but from the scarlet devils and the silver curve of fish—this, the cheese which he knew he smelled and the hermetic meat which his intestines believed he smelled coming in intermittent gusts momentary and brief between the other constant one, the smell and sense just a little of fear because mostly of despair and grief, the old fierce pull of blood. He could not see the table where the Justice sat and before which his father and his father's enemy *(our enemy* he thought in that despair; *ourn! mine and hisn both! He's my father!)* stood, but he could hear them, the two of them that is, because his father had said no word yet:

"But what proof have you, Mr. Harris?"

"I told you. The hog got into my corn. I caught it up and sent it back to him. He had no fence that would hold it. I told him so, warned him. The next time I put the hog in my pen. When he came to get it I gave him enough wire to patch up his pen. The next time I put the hog up and kept it. I rode down to his house and saw the wire I gave him still rolled on to the spool in his yard. I told him he could have the hog when he paid me a dollar pound fee. That evening a nigger came with the dollar and got the hog. He was a strange nigger. He said, 'He say to tell you wood and hay kin burn.' I said, 'What?' 'That whut he say to tell you,' the nigger said. 'Wood and hay kin burn.' That night my barn burned. I got the stock out but I lost the barn."

"Where is the nigger? Have you got him?"

"He was a strange nigger, I tell you. I don't know what became of him."

"But that's not proof. Don't you see that's not proof?"

"Get that boy up here. He knows." For a moment the boy thought too that the man meant his older brother until Harris said, "Not him. The little one. The boy," and, crouching, small for his age, small and wiry like his father, in patched and faded jeans even too small for him, with straight, uncombed, brown hair and eyes gray and wild as storm scud, he saw the men between himself and the table part and become a lane of grim faces, at the end of which he saw the Justice, a shabby, collarless, graying man in spectacles, beckoning him. He felt no floor under his bare feet; he seemed to walk beneath the palpable weight of the grim turning faces. His father, stiff in his black Sunday coat donned not for the trial but for the moving, did not even look at him. *He aims for me to lie,* he thought, again with that frantic grief and despair. *And I will have to do hit.*

"What's your name, boy?" the Justice said.

"Colonel Sartoris Snopes," the boy whispered.

"Hey?" the Justice said. "Talk louder. Colonel Sartoris? I reckon anybody named for Colonel Sartoris in this country can't help but tell the truth, can they?" The boy said nothing. *Enemy! Enemy!* he thought; for a moment he could not even see, could not see that the Justice's face was kindly nor discern that his voice was troubled when he spoke to the man named Harris: "Do you want me to question this boy?" But he could hear, and during those subsequent long seconds while there was absolutely no sound in the crowded little room save that of quiet and intent breathing it was as if he had swung outward at the end of a grape vine, over a ravine, and at the top of the swing had been caught in a prolonged instant of mesmerized gravity, weightless in time.

"No!" Harris said violently, explosively. "Damnation! Send him out of here!" Now time, the fluid world, rushed beneath him again, the voices coming to him again through the smell of cheese and sealed meat, the fear and despair and the old grief of blood:

"This case is closed. I can't find against you, Snopes, but I can give you advice. Leave this country and don't come back to it."

His father spoke for the first time, his voice cold and harsh, level, without emphasis: "I aim to. I don't figure to stay in a country among people who . . ." he said something unprintable and vile, addressed to no one.

"That'll do," the Justice said. "Take your wagon and get out of this country before dark. Case dismissed."

His father turned, and he followed the stiff black coat, the wiry figure walking a little stiffly from where a Confederate provost's man's musket ball had taken him in the heel on a stolen horse thirty years ago, followed the two backs now, since his older brother had appeared from somewhere in the crowd, no taller than the father but thicker, chewing tobacco steadily, between the two lines of grim-faced men and out of the store and across the worn gallery and down the sagging steps and among the dogs and half-grown boys in the mild May dust, where as he passed a voice hissed:

"Barn burner!"

Again he could not see, whirling; there was a face in a red haze, moonlike, bigger than the full moon, the owner of it half again his size, he leaping in the red haze toward the face, feeling no blow, feeling no shock when his head struck the earth, scrabbling up and leaping again, feeling no blow this time either and tasting no blood, scrabbling up to see the other boy in full flight and himself already leaping into pursuit as his father's hand jerked him back, the harsh, cold voice speaking above him: "Go get in the wagon."

It stood in a grove of locusts and mulberries across the road. His two hulking sisters in their Sunday dresses and his mother and her sister in calico and sunbonnets were already in it, sitting on and among the sorry residue of the dozen and more movings which even the boy could remember—the battered stove, the broken beds and chairs, the clock inlaid with mother-of-pearl, which would not run, stopped at some fourteen minutes past two o'clock of a dead and forgotten day and time, which had been his mother's dowry. She was crying, though when she saw him she drew her sleeve across her face and began to descend from the wagon. "Get back," the father said.

"He's hurt. I got to get some water and wash his . . ."

"Get back in the wagon," his father said. He got in too, over the tail-gate. His father mounted to the seat where the older brother already sat and struck the gaunt mules two savage blows with the peeled willow, but without heat. It was not even sadistic; it was exactly that same quality which in later years would cause his descendants to over-run the engine before putting a motor car into motion, striking and reining back in the same movement. The wagon went on, the store with its quiet crowd of grimly watching men dropped behind; a curve in the road hid it. *Forever* he thought. *Maybe he's done satisfied now, now that he has* . . . stopping himself, not to say it aloud even to himself. His mother's hand touched his shoulder.

"Does hit hurt?" she said.

"Naw," he said. "Hit don't hurt. Lemme be."

"Can't you wipe some of the blood off before hit dries?"

"I'll wash to-night," he said. "Lemme be, I tell you."

The wagon went on. He did not know where they were going. None of them ever did or ever asked, because it was always somewhere, always a house of sorts waiting for them a day or two days or even three days away. Likely his father had already arranged to make a crop on another farm before he . . . Again he had to stop himself. He (the father) always did. There was something about his wolflike independence and even courage when the advantage was at least neutral which impressed strangers, as if they got from his latent ravening ferocity not so much a sense of dependability as a feeling that his ferocious conviction in the rightness of his own actions would be of advantage to all whose interest lay with his.

That night they camped in a grove of oaks and beeches where a spring ran. The nights were still cool and they had a fire against it, of a rail lifted from a nearby fence and cut into lengths—a small fire, neat, niggard almost, a shrewd fire; such fires were his father's habit and custom always, even in freezing weather. Older, the boy might have remarked this and wondered why not a big one; why should not a man who had not only seen the waste and extravagance of war, but who had in his blood an inherent voracious prodigality with material not his own, have burned everything in sight? Then he might have gone a step farther and thought that that was the reason: that niggard blaze was the living fruit of nights passed during those four years in the woods hiding from all men, blue or gray, with his strings of horses (captured horses, he called them). And older still, he might have divined the true reason: that the element of fire spoke to some deep mainspring of his father's being, as the element of steel or of powder spoke to other men, as the one weapon for the preservation of integrity, else breath were not worth the breathing, and hence to be regarded with respect and used with discretion.

But he did not think this now and he had seen those same niggard blazes all his life. He merely ate his supper beside it and was already half asleep over his iron plate when his father called him, and once more he followed the stiff back, the stiff and ruthless limp, up the slope and on to the starlit road where, turning, he could see his father against the stars but without face or depth—a shape black, flat, and bloodless as though cut from tin in the iron folds of the frockcoat which had not been made for him, the voice harsh like tin and without heat like tin:

"You were fixing to tell them. You would have told him." He didn't answer. His father struck him with the flat of his hand on the side of the head, hard but without heat, exactly as he had struck the two mules at the store, exactly as he would strike either of them with any stick in order to kill a horse fly, his voice still without heat or anger: "You're getting to be a man. You got to learn. You got to learn to stick to your own blood or you ain't going to have any blood to stick to you. Do you think either of them, any man there this morning would? Don't you know all they wanted was a chance to get at me because they knew I had them beat? Eh?" Later, twenty years later, he was to tell himself, "If I had said they wanted only truth, justice, he would have hit me again." But now he said nothing. He was not crying. He just stood there. "Answer me," his father said.

"Yes," he whispered. His father turned.

"Get on to bed. We'll be there to-morrow."

To-morrow they were there. In the early afternoon the wagon stopped before a paintless two-room house identical almost with the dozen others it had stopped before even in the boy's ten years, and again, as on the other dozen occasions, his mother and aunt got down and began to unload the wagon, although his two sisters and his father and brother had not moved.

"Likely hit ain't fitten for hawgs," one of the sisters said.

"Nevertheless, fit it will and you'll hog it and like it," his father said. "Get out of them chairs and help your Ma unload."

The two sisters got down, big, bovine, in a flutter of cheap ribbons; one of them drew from the jumbled wagon bed a battered lantern, the other a worn broom. His father handed the reins to the older son and began to climb stiffly over the wheel. "When they get unloaded, take the team to the barn and feed them." Then he said, and at first the boy thought he was still speaking to his brother: "Come with me."

"Me?" he said.

"Yes," his father said. "You."

"Abner," his mother said. His father paused and looked back—the harsh level stare beneath the shaggy, graying, irascible brows.

"I reckon I'll have a word with the man that aims to begin to-morrow owning me body and soul for the next eight months."

They went back up the road. A week ago—or before last night, that is—he would have asked where they were going, but not now. His father had struck him before last night but never before had he paused afterward to explain why; it was as if the blow and the following calm, outrageous voice still rang, repercussed, divulging nothing to him save the terrible handicap of being young, the light weight of his few years, just heavy enough to prevent his soaring free of the world as it seemed to be ordered but not heavy enough to keep him footed solid in it, to resist it and try to change the course of its events.

Presently he could see the grove of oaks and cedars and the other flowering trees and shrubs where the house would be, though not the house yet. They walked beside a fence massed with honeysuckle and Cherokee roses and came to a gate swinging open between two brick pillars, and now, beyond a sweep of drive, he saw the house for the first time and at that instant he forgot his father and the terror and despair both, and even when he remembered his father again (who had not stopped) the terror and despair did not return. Because, for all the twelve movings, they had sojourned until now in a poor country, a land of small farms and fields and houses, and he had never seen a house like this before. *Hit's big as a courthouse* he thought quietly, with a surge of peace and joy whose reason he could not have thought into words, being too young for that: *They are safe from him. People whose lives are a part of this peace and dignity are beyond his touch, he no more to them than a buzzing wasp: capable of stinging for a little moment but that's all; the spell of this peace and dignity rendering even the barns and stable and cribs which belong to it impervious to the puny flames he might contrive* . . . this, the peace and joy, ebbing for an instant as he looked again at the stiff black back, the stiff and implacable limp of the figure which was not dwarfed by the house, for the reason that it had never looked big anywhere and which now, against the serene columned backdrop, had more than ever that impervious quality of something cut ruthlessly from tin, depthless, as though, sidewise to the sun, it would cast no shadow. Watching him, the boy remarked the absolutely undeviating course which his father held and saw the stiff foot come squarely down in a pile of fresh droppings where a horse had stood in the drive and which his father could have avoided by a simple change of stride. But it ebbed only for a moment, though he could not have thought this into words either, walking on in the spell of the house, which he could even want but without envy, without sorrow, certainly never with that ravening and jealous rage which unknown to him walked in the ironlike black coat before him. *Maybe he will feel it too. Maybe it will even change him now from what maybe he couldn't help but be.*

They crossed the portico. Now he could hear his father's stiff foot as it came down on the boards with clocklike finality, a sound out of all proportion to the displacement of the body it bore and which was not dwarfed either by the white door before it, as though it had attained to a sort of vicious and ravening minimum not to be dwarfed by anything—the flat, wide, black hat, the formal coat of broadcloth which had once been black but which had now the friction-glazed greenish cast of the bodies of old house flies, the lifted sleeve which was too large, the lifted hand like a curled claw. The door opened so promptly that the boy knew the Negro must have been watching them all the time, an old man with neat grizzled hair, in a linen jacket, who stood barring the door with his body, saying, "Wipe yo foots, white man, fo you come in here. Major ain't home nohow."

"Get out of my way, nigger," his father said, without heat too, flinging the door back and the Negro also and entering, his hat still on his head. And now the boy saw the prints of the stiff foot on the doorjamb and saw them appear on the pale rug behind the machinelike deliberation of the foot which seemed to bear (or transmit) twice the weight which the body compassed. The Negro was shouting "Miss Lula! Miss Lula!" somewhere behind them, then the boy, deluged as though by a warm wave by a suave turn of carpeted stair and a pendant glitter of chandeliers and a mute gleam of gold frames, heard the swift feet and saw her too, a lady—perhaps he had never seen her like before either—in a gray, smooth gown with lace at the throat and an apron tied at the waist and the sleeves turned back, wiping cake or biscuit dough from her hands with a towel as she came up the hall, looking not at his father at all but at the tracks on the blond rug with an expression of incredulous amazement.

"I tried," the Negro cried. "I tole him to . . ."

"Will you please go away?" she said in a shaking voice. "Major de Spain is not at home. Will you please go away?"

His father had not spoken again. He did not speak again. He did not even look at her. He just stood stiff in the center of the rug, in his hat, the shaggy iron-gray brows twitching slightly above the pebble-colored eyes as he appeared to examine the house with brief deliberation. Then with the same deliberation he turned; the boy watched him pivot on the good leg and saw the stiff foot drag round the arc of the turning, leaving a final long and fading smear. His father never looked at it, he never once looked down at the rug. The Negro held the door. It closed behind them, upon the hysteric and indistinguishable woman-wail. His father stopped at the top of the steps and scraped his boot clean on the edge of it. At the gate he stopped again. He stood for a moment, planted stiffly on the stiff foot, looking back at the house. "Pretty and white, ain't it?" he said. "That's sweat. Nigger sweat. Maybe it ain't white enough yet to suit him. Maybe he wants to mix some white sweat with it."

Two hours later the boy was chopping wood behind the house within which his mother and aunt and the two sisters (the mother and aunt, not the two girls, he knew that; even at this distance and muffled by walls the flat loud voices of the two girls emanated an incorrigible idle inertia) were setting up the stove to prepare a meal, when he heard the hooves and saw the linen-clad man on a fine sorrel mare, whom he recognized even before he saw the rolled rug in front of the Negro youth following on a fat bay carriage horse—a suffused, angry face vanishing, still at full gallop, beyond the corner of the house where his father and brother were sitting in the two tilted chairs; and a moment later, almost before he could have put the axe down, he heard the hooves again and watched the sorrel mare go back out of the yard, already galloping again. Then his father began to shout one of the sisters' names, who presently emerged backward from the kitchen door dragging the rolled rug along the ground by one end while the other sister walked behind it.

"If you ain't going to tote, go on and set up the wash pot," the first said.

"You, Sarty!" the second shouted, "Set up the wash pot!" His father appeared at the door, framed against that shabbiness, as he had been against that other bland perfection, impervious to either, the mother's anxious face at his shoulder.

"Go on," the father said. "Pick it up." The two sisters stooped, broad, lethargic; stooping, they presented an incredible expanse of pale cloth and a flutter of tawdry ribbons.

"If I thought enough of a rug to have to git hit all the way from France I wouldn't keep hit where folks coming in would have to tromp on hit," the first said. They raised the rug.

"Abner," the mother said. "Let me do it."

"You go back and git dinner," his father said. "I'll tend to this."

From the woodpile through the rest of the afternoon the boy watched them, the rug spread flat in the dust beside the bubbling wash-pot, the two sisters stooping over it with that profound and lethargic reluctance, while the father stood over them in turn, implacable and grim, driving them though never raising his voice again. He could smell the harsh homemade lye they were using; he saw his mother come to the door once and look toward them with an expression not anxious now but very like despair; he saw his father turn, and he fell to with the axe and saw from the corner of his eye his father raise from the ground a flattish fragment of field stone and examine it and return to the pot, and this time his mother actually spoke: "Abner. Abner. Please don't. Please, Abner."

Then he was done too. It was dusk; the whippoorwills had already begun. He could smell coffee from the room where they would presently eat the cold food remaining from the mid-afternoon meal, though when he entered the house he realized they were having coffee again probably because there was a fire on the hearth, before which the rug now lay spread over the backs of the two chairs. The tracks of his father's foot were gone. Where they had been were now long, water-cloudy scoriations resembling the sporadic course of a lilliputian mowing machine.

It still hung there while they ate the cold food and then went to bed, scattered without order or claim up and down the two rooms, his mother in one bed, where his father would later lie, the older brother in the other, himself, the aunt, and the two sisters on pallets on the floor. But his father was not in bed yet. The last thing the boy remembered was the depthless, harsh silhouette of the hat and coat bending over the rug and it seemed to him that he had not even closed his eyes when the silhouette was standing over him, the fire almost dead behind it, the stiff foot prodding him awake. "Catch up the mule," his father said.

When he returned with the mule his father was standing in the black door, the rolled rug over his shoulder. "Ain't you going to ride?" he said.

"No. Give me your foot."

He bent his knee into his father's hand, the wiry, surprising power flowed smoothly, rising, he rising with it, on to the mule's bare back (they had owned a saddle once; the boy could remember it though not when or where) and with the same effortlessness his father swung the rug up in front of him. Now in the starlight they retraced the afternoon's path, up the dusty road rife with honeysuckle, through the gate and up the black tunnel of the drive to the lightless house, where he sat on the mule and felt the rough warp of the rug drag across his thighs and vanish.

"Don't you want me to help?" he whispered. His father did not answer and now he heard again that stiff foot striking the hollow portico with that wooden and clocklike deliberation, that outrageous overstatement of the weight it carried. The rug, hunched, not flung (the boy could tell that even in the darkness) from his father's shoulder struck the angle of wall and floor with a sound unbelievably loud, thunderous, then the foot again, unhurried and enormous; a light came on in the house and the boy sat, tense, breathing steadily and quietly and just a little fast, though the foot itself did not increase its beat at all, descending the steps now; now the boy could see him.

"Don't you want to ride now?" he whispered. "We kin both ride now," the light within the house altering now, flaring up and sinking. *He's coming down the stairs now,* he thought. He had already ridden the mule up beside the horse block; presently his father was up behind him and he doubled the reins over and slashed the mule across the neck, but before the animal could begin to trot the hard, thin arm came round him, the hard, knotted hand jerking the mule back to a walk.

In the first red rays of the sun they were in the lot, putting plow gear on the mules. This time the sorrel mare was in the lot before he heard it at all, the rider collarless and even bareheaded, trembling, speaking in a shaking voice as the woman in the house had done, his father merely looking up once before stooping again to the hame he was buckling, so that the man on the mare spoke to his stooping back:

"You must realize you have ruined that rug. Wasn't there anybody here, any of your women . . ." he ceased, shaking, the boy watching him, the older brother leaning now in the stable door, chewing, blinking slowly and steadily at nothing apparently. "It cost a hundred dollars. But you never had a hundred dollars. You never will. So I'm going to charge you twenty bushels of corn against your crop. I'll add it in your contract and when you come to the commissary you can sign it. That won't keep Mrs. de Spain quiet but maybe it will teach you to wipe your feet off before you enter her house again."

Then he was gone. The boy looked at his father, who still had not spoken or even looked up again, who was now adjusting the logger-head in the hame.

"Pap," he said. His father looked at him—the inscrutable face, the shaggy brows beneath which the gray eyes glinted coldly. Suddenly the boy went toward him, fast, stopping as suddenly. "You done the best you could!" he cried. "If he wanted hit done different why didn't he wait and tell you how? He won't git no twenty bushels! He won't git none! We'll gether hit and hide hit! I kin watch . . ."

"Did you put the cutter back in that straight stock like I told you?"

"No sir," he said.

"Then go do it."

That was Wednesday. During the rest of that week he worked steadily, at what was within his scope and some which was beyond it, with an industry that did not need to be driven nor even commanded twice; he had this from his mother, with the difference that some at least of what he did he liked to do, such as splitting wood with the half-size axe which his mother and aunt had earned, or saved money somehow, to present him with at Christmas. In company with the two older women (and on one afternoon, even one of the sisters), he built pens for the shoat and the cow which were a part of his father's contract with the landlord, and one afternoon, his father being absent, gone somewhere on one of the mules, he went to the field.

They were running a middle buster now, his brother holding the plow straight while he handled the reins, and walking beside the straining mule, the rich black soil shearing cool and damp against his bare ankles, he thought *Maybe this is the end of it. Maybe even that twenty bushels that seems hard to have to pay for just a rug will be a cheap price for him to stop forever and always from being what he used to be;* thinking, dreaming now, so that his brother had to speak sharply to him to mind the mule: *Maybe he even won't collect the twenty bushels. Maybe it will all add up and balance and vanish—corn, rug, fire; the terror and grief, the being pulled two ways like between two teams of horses—gone, done with for ever and ever.*

Then it was Saturday; he looked up from beneath the mule he was harnessing and saw his father in the black coat and hat. "Not that," his father said. "The wagon gear." And then, two hours later, sitting in the wagon bed behind his father and brother on the seat, the wagon accomplished a final curve, and he saw the weathered paintless store with its tattered tobacco and patent-medicine posters and the tethered wagons and saddle animals below the gallery. He mounted the gnawed steps behind his father and brother, and there again was the lane of quiet, watching faces for the three of them to walk through. He saw the man in spectacles sitting at the plank table and he did not need to be told this was a Justice of the Peace; he sent one glare of fierce, exultant, partisan defiance at the man in collar and cravat now, whom he had seen but twice before in his life, and that on a galloping horse, who now wore on his face an expression not of rage but of amazed unbelief which the boy could not have known was at the incredible circumstance of being sued by one of his own tenants, and came and stood against his father and cried at the Justice: "He ain't done it! He ain't burnt . . ."

"Go back to the wagon," his father said.

"Burnt?" the Justice said. "Do I understand this rug was burned too?"

"Does anybody here claim it was?" his father said. "Go back to the wagon." But he did not, he merely retreated to the rear of the room, crowded as that other had been, but not to sit down this time, instead, to stand pressing among the motionless bodies, listening to the voices:

"And you claim twenty bushels of corn is too high for the damage you did to the rug?"

"He brought the rug to me and said he wanted the tracks washed out of it. I washed the tracks out and took the rug back to him."

"But you didn't carry the rug back to him in the same condition it was in before you made the tracks on it."

His father did not answer, and now for perhaps half a minute there was no sound at all save that of breathing, the faint, steady suspiration of complete and intent listening.

"You decline to answer that, Mr. Snopes?" Again his father did not answer. "I'm going to find against you, Mr. Snopes. I'm going to find that you were responsible for the injury to Major de Spain's rug and hold you liable for it. But twenty bushels of corn seems a little high for a man in your circumstances to have to pay. Major de Spain claims it cost a hundred dollars. October corn will be worth about fifty cents. I figure that if Major de Spain can stand a ninety-five dollar loss on something he paid cash for, you can stand a five-dollar loss you haven't earned yet. I hold you in damages to Major de Spain to the amount of ten bushels of corn over and above your contract with him, to be paid to him out of your crop at gathering time. Court adjourned."

It had taken no time hardly, the morning was but half begun. He thought they would return home and perhaps back to the field, since they were late, far behind all other farmers. But instead his father passed on behind the wagon, merely indicating with his hand for the older brother to follow with it, and he crossed the road toward the blacksmith shop opposite, pressing on after his father, overtaking him, speaking, whispering up at the harsh, calm face beneath the weathered hat: "He won't git no ten bushels neither. He won't git one. We'll . . ." until his father glanced for an instant down at him, the face absolutely calm, the grizzled eyebrows tangled above the cold eyes, the voice almost pleasant, almost gentle:

"You think so? Well, we'll wait till October anyway."

The matter of the wagon—the setting of a spoke or two and the tightening of the tires—did not take long either, the business of the tires accomplished by driving the wagon into the spring branch behind the shop and letting it stand there, the mules nuzzling into the water from time to time, and the boy on the seat with the idle reins, looking up the slope and through the sooty tunnel of the shed where the slow hammer rang and where his father sat on an upended cypress bolt, easily, either talking or listening, still sitting there when the boy brought the dripping wagon up out of the branch and halted it before the door.

"Take them on to the shade and hitch," his father said. He did so and returned. His father and the smith and a third man squatting on his heels inside the door were talking, about crops and animals; the boy, squatting too in the ammoniac dust and hoof-parings and scales of rust, heard his father tell a long and unhurried story out of the time before the birth of the older brother even when he had been a professional horsetrader. And then his father came up beside him where he stood before a tattered last year's circus poster on the other side of the store, gazing rapt and quiet at the scarlet horses, the incredible poisings and convolutions of tulle and tights and the painted leer of comedians, and said, "It's time to eat."

But not at home. Squatting beside his brother against the front wall, he watched his father emerge from the store and produce from a paper sack a segment of cheese and divide it carefully and deliberately into three with his pocket knife and produce crackers from the same sack. They all three squatted on the gallery and ate, slowly, without talking; then in the store again, they drank from a tin dipper tepid water smelling of the cedar bucket and of living beech trees. And still they did not go home. It was a horse lot this time, a tall rail fence upon and along which men stood and sat and out of which one by one horses were led, to be walked and trotted and then cantered back and forth along the road while the slow swapping and buying went on and the sun began to slant westward, they—the three of them—watching and listening, the older brother with his muddy eyes and his steady, inevitable tobacco, the father commenting now and then on certain of the animals, to no one in particular.

It was after sundown when they reached home. They ate supper by lamplight, then, sitting on the doorstep, the boy watched the night fully accomplished, listening to the whippoorwills and the frogs, when he heard his mother's voice: "Abner! No! No! Oh, God. Oh, God. Abner!" and he rose, whirled, and saw the altered light through the door where a candle stub now burned in a bottle neck on the table and his father, still in the hat and coat, at once formal and burlesque as though dressed carefully for some shabby and ceremonial violence, emptying the reservoir of the lamp back into the five-gallon kerosene can from which it had been filled, while the mother tugged at his arm until he shifted the lamp to the other hand and flung her back, not savagely or viciously, just hard, into the wall, her hands flung out against the wall for balance, her mouth open and in her face the same quality of hopeless despair as had been in her voice. Then his father saw him standing in the door.

"Go to the barn and get that can of oil we were oiling the wagon with," he said. The boy did not move. Then he could speak.

"What . . ." he cried "What are you . . ."

"Go get that oil," his father said. "Go."

Then he was moving, running outside the house, toward the stable: this the old habit, the old blood which he had not been permitted to choose for himself, which had been bequeathed him willy nilly and which had run for so long (and who knew where, battening on what of outrage and savagery and lust) before it came to him. *I could keep on,* he thought. *I could run on and on and never look back, never need to see his face again. Only I can't. I can't,* the rusted can in his hand now, the liquid sploshing in it as he ran back to the house and into it, into the sound of his mother's weeping in the next room, and handed the can to his father.

"Ain't you going to even send a nigger?" he cried. "At least you sent a nigger before!"

This time his father didn't strike him. The hand came even faster than the blow had, the same hand which had set the can on the table with almost excruciating care flashing from the can toward him too quick for him to follow it, gripping him by the back of the shirt and on to tiptoe before he had seen it quit the can, the face stooping at him in breathless and frozen ferocity, the cold, dead voice speaking over him to the older brother who leaned against the table, chewing with that steady, curious, sidewise motion of cows:

"Empty the can into the big one and go on. I'll ketch up with you."

"Better tie him to the bedpost," the brother said.

"Do like I told you," the father said. Then the boy was moving, his bunched shirt and the hard, bony hand between his shoulder-blades, his toes just touching the floor, across the room and into the other one, past the sisters sitting with spread heavy thighs in the two chairs over the cold hearth, and to where his mother and aunt sat side by side on the bed, the aunt's arms about his mother's shoulders.

"Hold him," the father said. The aunt made a startled movement. "Not you," the father said. "Lennie. Take hold of him. I want to see you do it." His mother took him by the wrist. "You'll hold him better than that. If he gets loose don't you know what he is going to do? He will go up yonder." He jerked his head toward the road. "Maybe I'd better tie him."

"I'll hold him," his mother whispered.

"See you do then." Then his father was gone, the stiff foot heavy and measured upon the boards, ceasing at last.

Then he began to struggle. His mother caught him in both arms, he jerking and wrenching at them. He would be stronger in the end, he knew that. But he had no time to wait for it. "Lemme go!" he cried. "I don't want to have to hit you!"

"Let him go!" the aunt said. "If he don't go, before God, I am going up there myself!"

"Don't you see I can't?" his mother cried. "Sarty! Sarty! No! No! Help me, Lizzie!"

Then he was free. His aunt grasped at him but was too late. He whirled, running, his mother stumbled forward on to her knees behind him, crying to the nearer sister: "Catch him, Net! Catch him!" But that was too late too, the sister (the sisters were twins, born at the same time, yet either of them now gave the impression of being, encompassing as much living meat and volume and weight as any other two of the family) not yet having begun to rise from the chair, her head, face, alone merely turned, presenting to him in the flying instant an astonishing expanse of young female features untroubled by any surprise even, wearing only an expression of bovine interest. Then he was out of the room, out of the house, in the mild dust of the starlit road and the heavy rifeness of honeysuckle, the pale ribbon unspooling with terrific slowness under his running feet, reaching the gate at last and turning in, running, his heart and lungs drumming, on up the drive toward the lighted house, the lighted door. He did not knock, he burst in, sobbing for breath, incapable for the moment of speech; he saw the astonished face of the Negro in the linen jacket without knowing when the Negro had appeared.

"De Spain!" he cried, panted. "Where's . . ." then he saw the white man too emerging from a white door down the hall. "Barn!" he cried. "Barn!"

"What?" the white man said. "Barn?"

"Yes!" the boy cried. "Barn!"

"Catch him!" the white man shouted.

But it was too late this time too. The Negro grasped his shirt, but the entire sleeve, rotten with washing, carried away, and he was out that door too and in the drive again, and had actually never ceased to run even while he was screaming into the white man's face.

Behind him the white man was shouting, "My horse! Fetch my horse!" and he thought for an instant of cutting across the park and climbing the fence into the road, but he did not know the park nor how high the vine-massed fence might be and he dared not risk it. So he ran on down the drive, blood and breath roaring; presently he was in the road again though he could not see it. He could not hear either: the galloping mare was almost upon him before he heard her, and even then he held his course, as if the urgency of his wild grief and need must in a moment more find him wings, waiting until the ultimate instant to hurl himself aside and into the weed-choked roadside ditch as the horse thundered past and on, for an instant in furious silhouette against the stars, the tranquil early summer night sky which, even before the shape of the horse and rider vanished, strained abruptly and violently upward: a long, swirling roar incredible and soundless, blotting the stars, and he springing up and into the road again, running again, knowing it was too late yet still running even after he heard the shot and, an instant later, two shots, pausing now without knowing he had ceased to run, crying "Pap! Pap!," running again before he knew he had begun to run, stumbling, tripping over something and scrabbling up again without ceasing to run, looking backward over his shoulder at the glare as he got up, running on among the invisible trees, panting, sobbing, "Father! Father!"

At midnight he was sitting on the crest of a hill. He did not know it was midnight and he did not know how far he had come. But there was no glare behind him now and he sat now, his back toward what he had called home for four days anyhow, his face toward the dark woods which he would enter when breath was strong again, small, shaking steadily in the chill darkness, hugging himself into the remainder of his thin, rotten shirt, the grief and despair now no longer terror and fear but just grief and despair. *Father. My father,* he thought. "He was brave!" he cried suddenly, aloud but not loud, no more than a whisper: "He was! He was in the war! He was in Colonel Sartoris' cav'ry!" not knowing that his father had gone to that war a private in the fine old European sense, wearing no uniform, admitting the authority of and giving fidelity to no man or army or flag, going to war as Malbrouck himself did: for booty—it meant nothing and less than nothing to him if it were enemy booty or his own.

The slow constellations wheeled on. It would be dawn and then sun-up after a while and he would be hungry. But that would be to-morrow and now he was only cold, and walking would cure that. His breathing was easier now and he decided to get up and go on, and then he found that he had been asleep because he knew it was almost dawn, the night almost over. He could tell that from the whippoorwills. They were everywhere now among the dark trees below him, constant and inflectioned and ceaseless, so that, as the instant for giving over to the day birds drew nearer and nearer, there was no interval at all between them. He got up. He was a little stiff, but walking would cure that too as it would the cold, and soon there would be the sun. He went on down the hill, toward the dark woods within which the liquid silver voices of the birds called unceasing—the rapid and urgent beating of the urgent and quiring heart of the late spring night. He did not look back.

Interpretive Questions

1. Why does Snopes burn the barns, and not the houses, of the men he works for?
2. Why are all the father's actions, even the violent ones, performed without emotion?
3. Why are the Justices of the Peace shown to be fair, decent men?
4. Why does Sarty warn Major de Spain?
5. Does Sarty overcome "the old fierce pull of blood"?

IV

By and About John Locke

(1632–1704)

When John Locke was fifty-seven, he still had not published a word of his writings. Then, within four years, he published four works that brought him recognition in his lifetime and lasting fame as one of England's greatest philosophers: *A Letter Concerning Toleration*, *Two Treatises of Government*, *An Essay Concerning Human Understanding*, and *Some Thoughts Concerning Education*.

Locke said there are three faults that inhibit our thinking:

> The first is of those who seldom reason at all, but do and think according to the example of others . . . for the saving of themselves the pains and trouble of thinking and examining for themselves. The second is of those who put passion in the place of reason, . . . and these one may observe commonly content themselves with words, which have no distinct ideas to them, though in other matters that they come with an unbiased indifferency to, they want not abilities to talk and hear reason. . . . The third sort is of those who readily and sincerely follow reason, but for want of having that which one may call large, sound, round-about sense have not a full view of all that relates to the question. . . . We are all short-sighted and often see but one side of a matter; our views are not extended to all that has a connection with it. From this defect I think no man is free.

He wrote about the difficulty of defining common terms:

> Any one almost would take it for an affront to be asked what he meant by [life]. And yet if it comes in question whether a plant that lies ready formed in the seed live, whether the embryo in an egg before incubation, or a man in a swoon without sense or motion be alive or no, it is easy to perceive that a clear, distinct, settled idea does not always accompany the use of so known a word as that of life is.

On doubting everything:

If we will disbelieve everything because we cannot certainly know all things, we shall do muchwhat as wisely as he who would not use his legs, but sit still and perish because he had no wings to fly.

On education:

The great skill of a teacher is to get and keep the attention of his scholar. . . . To attain this, he should make the child comprehend, as much as may be, the usefulness of what he teaches him and let him see, by what he has learned, that he can do something which gives him some power and real advantage over others who are ignorant of it.

I confess there are some men's constitutions of body and mind so vigorous and well framed by nature that they need not much assistance from others, but by the strength of their natural genius they are from their cradles carried towards what is excellent, and by the privilege of their happy constitutions are able to do wonders. But examples of this kind are but few, and I think I may say that of all the men we meet with, nine parts of ten are what they are, good or evil, useful or not, by their education. 'Tis that which makes the great difference of mankind.

Locke's First Treatise of Government *is a refutation of the divine right of kings. In it, he argues that God did not place some people over others—fathers over sons, men over women, kings over subjects—but that all people are equal. In the* Second Treatise, *from which our selection is taken, Locke presents his conception of civil government: People unite under a government in order to live comfortably and peacefully. In the state of nature that precedes political society, they are free to live as they see fit, to enjoy their possessions, and to punish those who harm or rob them; but since others are equally free, no one can be secure. Therefore, people are willing to give up some of their freedom to government as long as its political power—its right to make and enforce laws—preserves their lives, liberties, and possessions better than they can independently.*

Of Civil Government

John Locke

Of the State of Nature

To understand political power aright, and derive it from its original, we must consider what state all men are naturally in, and that is a state of perfect freedom to order their actions and dispose of their possessions and persons as they think fit, within the bounds of the law of nature, without asking leave, or depending upon the will of any other man.

A state also of equality, wherein all the power and jurisdiction is reciprocal, no one having more than another; there being nothing more evident than that creatures of the same species and rank, promiscuously born to all the same advantages of nature, and the use of the same faculties, should also be equal one amongst another without subordination or subjection. . . .

But though this be a state of liberty, yet it is not a state of license; though man in that state have an uncontrollable liberty to dispose of his person or possessions, yet he has not liberty

---

*A selection from *Second Treatise of Government.*

to destroy himself, or so much as any creature in his possession, but where some nobler use than its bare preservation calls for it. The state of nature has a law of nature to govern it, which obliges every one; and reason, which is that law, teaches all mankind who will but consult it, that, being all equal and independent, no one ought to harm another in his life, health, liberty, or possessions. For men being all the workmanship of one omnipotent and infinitely wise Maker . . . there cannot be supposed any such subordination among us that may authorize us to destroy one another, as if we were made for one another's uses, as the inferior ranks of creatures are for ours. Every one, as he is bound to preserve himself, and not to quit his station willfully, so, by the like reason, when his own preservation comes not in competition, ought he, as much as he can, to preserve the rest of mankind, and not, unless it be to do justice on an offender, take away or impair the life, or what tends to the preservation of the life, the liberty, health, limb, or goods of another. . . .

To those that say there were never any men in the state of nature, I . . . affirm that all men are naturally in that state, and remain so, till by their own consents they make themselves members of some politic society; and I doubt not, in the sequel of this discourse, to make it very clear. . . .

Of the Ends of Political Society and Government

If man in the state of nature be so free, as has been said, if he be absolute lord of his own person and possessions, equal to the greatest, and subject to nobody, why will he part with his freedom, this empire, and subject himself to the dominion and control of any other power? To which, it is obvious to answer, that though in the state of nature he hath such a right, yet the enjoyment of it is very uncertain, and constantly exposed to the invasions of others. For all being kings as much as he, every man his equal, and the greater part no strict observers of equity and justice, the enjoyment of the property he has in this state is very unsafe, very unsecure. This makes him willing to quit this condition, which, however free, is full of fears and continual dangers; and it is not without reason that he seeks out and is willing to join in society with others, who are already united, or have a mind to unite, for the mutual preservation of their lives, liberties, and estates, which I call by the general name, property.

The great and chief end, therefore, of men's uniting into commonwealths, and putting themselves under government, is the preservation of their property; to which in the state of nature there are many things wanting.

First, there wants an established, settled, known law, received and allowed by common consent to be the standard of right and wrong, and the common measure to decide all controversies between them. For though the law of nature be plain and intelligible to all rational creatures, yet men, being biased by their interest, as well as ignorant for want of study of it, are not apt to allow of it as a law binding to them in the application of it to their particular cases.

Secondly, in the state of nature there wants a known and indifferent judge, with authority to determine all differences according to the established law. For every one in that state being both judge and executioner of the law of nature, men being partial to themselves, passion and revenge is very apt to carry them too far, and with too much heat in their own cases, as well as negligence and unconcernedness, to make them too remiss in other men's.

Thirdly, in the state of nature there often wants power to back and support the sentence when right, and to give it due execution. They who by any injustice offend will seldom fail, where they are able by force to make good their injustice; such resistance many times makes the punishment dangerous, and frequently destructive to those who attempt it.

Thus mankind, notwithstanding all the privileges of the state of nature, being but in an ill condition while they remain in it, are quickly driven into society. Hence it comes to pass that we seldom find any number of men live any time together in this state. The inconveniences that they are therein exposed to by the irregular and uncertain exercise of the power every man has of punishing the transgressions of others, make them take sanctuary under the established laws of government, and therein seek the preservation of their property. It is this makes them so willingly give up every one his single power of punishing, to be exercised by such alone as shall be appointed to it amongst them, and by such rules as the community, or those authorized by them to that purpose, shall agree on. And in this we have the original right and rise of both the legislative and executive power, as well as of the governments and societies themselves.

For in the state of nature, to omit the liberty he has of innocent delights, a man has two powers.

The first is to do whatsoever he thinks fit for the preservation of himself, and others within the permission of the law of nature, by which law, common to them all, he and all the rest of mankind are of one community, make up one society, distinct from all other creatures. And were it not for the corruption and viciousness of degenerate men there would be no need of any other, no necessity that men should separate from this great and natural community, and associate into lesser combinations.

The other power a man has in the state of nature is the

power to punish the crimes committed against that law. Both these he gives up when he joins in a private, if I may so call it, or particular political society, and incorporates into any commonwealth separate from the rest of mankind.

The first power, viz., of doing whatsoever he thought fit for the preservation of himself and the rest of mankind, he gives up to be regulated by laws made by the society, so far forth as the preservation of himself and the rest of that society shall require; which laws of the society in many things confine the liberty he had by the law of nature.

Secondly, the power of punishing he wholly gives up, and engages his natural force (which he might before employ in the execution of the law of nature by his own single authority as he thought fit) to assist the executive power of the society, as the law thereof shall require. For being now in a new state, wherein he is to enjoy many conveniences from the labor, assistance, and society of others in the same community, as well as protection from its whole strength; he has to part also with as much of his natural liberty, in providing for himself, as the good, prosperity and safety of the society shall require; which is not only necessary but just, since the other members of the society do the like.

But though men when they enter into society give up the equality, liberty and executive power they had in the state of nature into the hands of the society, to be so far disposed of by the legislative as the good of the society shall require; yet it being only with an intention in every one the better to preserve himself, his liberty and property (for no rational creature can be supposed to change his condition with an intention to be worse), the power of the society, or legislative constituted by them, can never be supposed to extend farther than the common good, but is obliged to secure every one's property by providing against those three defects above mentioned that made the state of nature so unsafe and uneasy. And so whoever has the legislative or supreme power of any commonwealth is bound to govern by established standing laws, promulgated and known to the people, and not by extemporary decrees; by indifferent and upright judges, who are to decide controversies by those laws; and to employ the force of the community at home only in the execution of such laws, or abroad to prevent or redress foreign injuries and secure the community from inroad and invasion. And all this to be directed to no other end but the peace, safety, and public good of the people.

Interpretive Questions

1. When an individual joins a commonwealth, does he give up any of the equality he had in the state of nature?
2. Does obeying the law of nature depend upon the belief that we are created by God?
3. Why does Locke think that we must consider what human beings are like in the state of nature in order to understand political power?
4. Why does Locke say that reason and the law of nature are the same?
5. Is preserving property the chief purpose of the commonwealth?

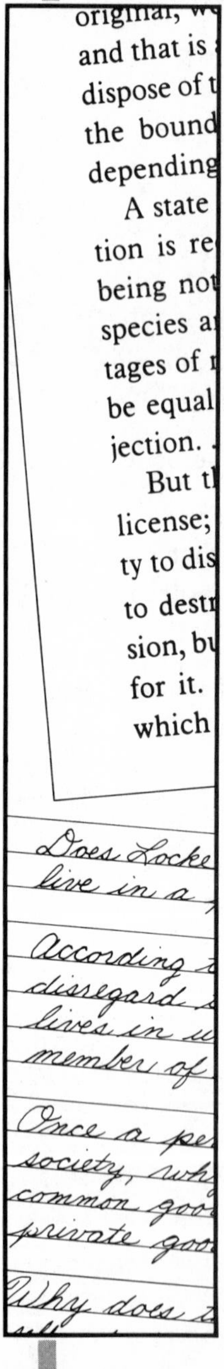

Preparing for Discussion

The Great Books program is based on shared inquiry—the gradual unfolding of meaning that occurs when readers explore a story or essay in discussion. Shared inquiry cannot take place unless all participants have immersed themselves in the material and come to terms with it in their various individual ways. This kind of involvement teaches us to trust our own responses and to use them as the basis for interpretation.

Discussion should be a free exchange of ideas and a process of discovery. If you are seriously attentive to a good story or essay, you will come to discussion eager to share your ideas. During discussion you will feel less concern about being "right" or "wrong" than you will about increasing your understanding of the material itself.

As part of your preparation for discussion, read each selection at least twice, with a pen or pencil in hand, and make notes of your thoughts and feelings as you read. Your notes may take any form you like: underline a passage, put a question mark above a line, jot down a comment in the margin. If you are not allowed to mark your book, there are other ways to make notations: clip a note to an important page, use removable self-stick notes, or jot down your thoughts about a selection in a notebook reserved for the Great Books program. If you keep a special notebook, place a page number next to each note so that you can quickly refer to the passage on which the note is based.

On your first reading, make a note of what you don't understand, what seems important, and what you agree or disagree with. What you note, or the number of notes you make, doesn't matter; the very act of making notes will help you get involved with the material and begin thinking about it.

On a second reading you will find yourself making new notes, and probably more of them, simply because you have read the entire selection once before. New passages will strike you as important now that you know how the selection ends. You will discover connections between passages that you had missed on your first reading: the repetition of a significant word or phrase, a pattern of ideas or actions, or something in the beginning of a selection that prepares you for the ending. You may also begin to see how the different parts fit together and why the author uses certain phrases.

Having completed both readings, you should review your notes and try to turn some of them into questions that you would like the group's help in answering. It may be appropriate to raise these questions during discussion of the leader's questions, or the leader may set aside a separate time for them.

The following example shows how one student took notes on a passage from the selection you have just read.

> To understand political power aright, and
> *original = source* — derive it from its original, we must consider what state all men are naturally in, and that is a state of perfect freedom to order their actions and dispose of their possessions and persons as they think fit, within the bounds of the law of nature, without asking leave, or depending upon the will of any other man.
>
> A state also of equality, wherein all the
> *NO!!* — power and jurisdiction is reciprocal, no one having more than another; there being nothing more evident than that creatures of the
> *rank?* — same species and rank, promiscuously born to all the same advantage of nature, and the use of the same faculties, should also be equal one
> *Isn't subordination sometimes natural?* — amongst another without subordination or subjection. . . .

V

Getting Into a Story

In our daily lives we often have to act before we understand; there is seldom time for simply feeling or seeing. But a story provides an opportunity for such reflection and a release from our usual responsibilities. It invites us to step outside ourselves—to set aside our prejudices and opinions and see what the world looks like from another angle of vision.

As we read a story, we observe the characters in their most private moments. We eavesdrop on their conversations and learn their innermost thoughts. Yet they pay us no mind, and no matter how intense our involvement, we never quite forget that they exist in a realm beyond our help. Since we stand neither to gain nor to lose by what goes on in a story, we can suspend judgment in favor of understanding. Reading a story is a way to participate, without risk, in another world.

Before we can enter the world of a story, we must first bring it to life in our minds. Envisioning a story—recreating an author's world in our own imagination—begins with an alertness to details and a sensuous or artistic appreciation of them. The details of a story guide reflection, anchoring our thoughts and feelings. They also serve, with our assistance, to bring characters and scenes to life.

Since writers seldom spell everything out for their readers, getting into a story involves not only collecting details, but a process of inference as well. For example, it would be a pointless exercise for even a very talented writer to attempt to describe a character completely. What he does instead is give us the most revealing or meaningful details. In fiction, the salient features of a face are apt to correspond to a character's inner world or to suggest something of his meaning for an author. With repetition and emphasis, physical facts may take on symbolic value.

In the best stories, each detail is carefully chosen not only for its power to evoke reality, but also as a guide to meaningful reflection. Our first priority, then, is to gather the "sunny trifles" of the story—to savor its concrete details. Through them the world of the story comes into being: the atmosphere builds and the shadowy figures of the author's imagination take on flesh. If these characters and their world possess what a poet called a "semblance of truth and sufficient human interest," they win our credence, or a "willing suspension of disbelief for the moment." Then we cease to be aware of the effort we are expending as we read. Our curiosity carries us through the story, which we read with passion and understanding. ■■

By and About Anton Chekhov

(1860–1904)

Anton Chekhov was born in Taganrog, a provincial port in southern Russia. He attended medical school at the University of Moscow, and after graduating, divided his time between medicine and writing. Looking back on his childhood, he once suggested it as material for a short story:

> Write a story, do, about a young man, the son of a serf, a former grocery boy, a choirsinger, a high school pupil and university student, brought up to respect rank, to kiss the hands of priests, to truckle to the ideas of others—a young man who expressed thanks for every piece of bread, who was whipped many times, who went without galoshes to do his tutoring, who used his fists, tortured animals, was fond of dining with rich relatives, was a hypocrite in his dealings with God and men, needlessly, solely out of a realization of his own insignificance—write how this young man squeezes the slave out of himself, drop by drop, and how, on awaking one fine morning, he feels that the blood coursing through his veins is no longer that of a slave but that of a real human being.

When criticized because his plays were not dramatic enough, he replied with a comment that also applies to his stories:

> In real life, people don't spend every minute shooting at each other, hanging themselves, and making confessions of love. They don't spend all the time saying clever things. They're more occupied with eating, drinking, flirting, and talking stupidities—and these are the things which ought to be shown on the stage. A play should be written in which people arrive, go away, have dinner, talk about the weather, and play cards. Life must be exactly as it is, and people as they are—not on stilts. . . . Let everything on the stage be just as complicated, and at the same time just as simple, as it is in life. People eat their dinner, just eat their dinner, and all the time their happiness is being established or their lives are being broken up.

His contemporary, Maxim Gorky, felt that no one understood the tragedy of life's trivialities as clearly and finely as Chekhov did. Gorky wrote:

> There passes before one a long file of men and women, slaves of their love, of their stupidity and idleness, of their greed for the good things of life; there walk the slaves of the dark fear of life; they struggle anxiously along, filling life with incoherent words about the future, feeling that in the present there is no place for them. . . .
>
> Many of them have nice dreams of how pleasant life will be in three hundred years, but it occurs to none of them to ask themselves who will make life pleasant if we only dream.
>
> In front of that dreary, gray crowd of helpless people there passed a great, wise, and observant man; he looked at all these dreary inhabitants of his country, and, with a sad smile, with a tone of gentle but deep reproach, with anguish in his face and in his heart, in a beautiful and sincere voice, he said to them:
>
> "You live badly, my friends. It is shameful to live like that."

In Exile

Anton Chekhov

Old Semyon, whose nickname was Preacher, and a young Tartar, whose name no one knew, were sitting by a campfire on the bank of the river; the other three ferrymen were inside the hut. Semyon, a gaunt, toothless old man of sixty, broad-shouldered and still healthy-looking, was drunk; he would have gone to bed long ago, but he had a bottle in his pocket and was afraid his comrades in the hut would ask him for a drink of vodka. The Tartar was worn out and ill, and, wrapping himself in his rags, he talked about how good it was in the province of Simbirsk, and what a beautiful and clever wife he had left at home. He was not more than twenty-five, and in the firelight his pale, sickly face and woebegone expression made him seem like a boy.

"Well, this is no paradise, of course," said Preacher. "You can see for yourself; water, bare banks, nothing but clay wherever you look. . . . It's long past Easter and there's still ice on the river . . . and this morning there was snow."

"Bad! Bad!" said the Tartar, surveying the landscape with dismay.

A few yards away the dark, cold river flowed, growling and sluicing against the pitted clay banks as it sped on to the distant sea. At the edge of the bank loomed a capacious barge, which ferrymen call a *karbas.* Far away on the opposite bank crawling snakes of fire were dying down then reappearing—last year's grass being burned. Beyond the snakes there was darkness again. Little blocks of ice could be heard knocking against the barge. It was cold and damp. . . .

The Tartar glanced at the sky. There were as many stars as there were at home, the same blackness, but something was lacking. At home, in the province of Simbirsk, the stars and the sky seemed altogether different.

"Bad! Bad!" he repeated.

"You'll get used to it!" said Preacher with a laugh. "You're still young and foolish—the milk's hardly dry on your lips—and in your foolishness you think there's no one more unfortunate than you, but the time will come when you'll say to yourself: may God give everyone such a life. Just look at me. In a week's time the floods will be over and we'll launch the ferry; you'll all go gadding about Siberia, while I stay here, going back and forth, from one bank to the other. For twenty-two years now that's what I've been doing. Day and night. The pike and the salmon under the water and me on it. That's all I want. God give everyone such a life."

The Tartar threw some brushwood onto the fire, lay down closer to it, and said, "My father is sick man. When he dies, my mother, my wife, will come here. Have promised."

"And what do you want a mother and a wife for?" asked Preacher. "Just foolishness, brother. It's the devil stirring you up, blast his soul! Don't listen to him, the Evil One! Don't give in to him. When he goes on about women, spite him: I don't want them! When he talks to you about freedom, you stand up to him: I don't want it! I want nothing! No father, no mother, no wife, no freedom, no house nor home! I want nothing, damn their souls!"

Preacher took a swig at the bottle and went on, "I'm no simple peasant, brother; I don't come from the servile class; I'm a deacon's son, and when I was free I lived in Kursk, and used to go around in a frock coat; but now I've brought myself to such a point that I can sleep naked on the ground and eat grass. And God give everyone such a life. I don't want anything, I'm not afraid of anyone, and the way I see it, there's no man richer or freer than I am. When they sent me here from Russia, from the very first day I jibbed: I want nothing! The devil was at me about my wife, about my kin, about freedom, but I told him: I want nothing! And I stuck to it; and here, you see, I live well, I don't complain. But if anyone humors the devil and listens to him even once, he's lost, no salvation for him. He'll be stuck fast in the bog, up to his ears, and he'll never get out.

"It's not only the likes of you, foolish peasants, that are lost, but even the well-born and educated. Fifteen years ago they sent a gentleman here from Russia. He forged a will or something—wouldn't share with his brothers. It was said he was a prince or a baron, but maybe he was only an official, who knows? Well, the gentleman came here, and the first thing, he bought himself a house and land in Mukhortinskoe. 'I want to live by my own labor,' says he, 'in the sweat of my brow, because I'm no longer a gentleman, but an exile.' . . . 'Well,' says I, 'may God help you, that's the right thing.' He was a young man then, a hustler, always on the move; he used to do the mowing himself, catch fish, ride sixty versts on horseback. But here was the trouble: from the very first year he began riding to Gyrino to the post office. He used to stand on my ferry and sigh, 'Ah, Semyon, for a long time now they haven't sent me any money from home.' . . . 'You don't need money, Vasily Sergeich. What good is it? Throw off the past, forget it as if it had never happened, as if it was only a dream, and start life afresh. Don't listen to the devil,' I tell him, 'he'll bring you to no good; he'll tighten the noose. Now you want money,' says I, 'and in a little while, before you know it, you'll want something else, and then more and more. But,' says I, 'if you want to be happy, the very first thing is not to want anything.' Yes. . . . 'And if fate has cruelly wronged you and me,' says I, 'it's no good going down on your knees to her and asking her favor; you have to spurn her and laugh at her, otherwise she'll laugh at you.' That's what I said to him. . . .

"Two years later I ferried him over to this side, and he was rubbing his hands together and laughing. 'I'm going to Gyrino,' says he, 'to meet my wife. She has taken pity on me and come here. She's so kind and good!' He was panting with joy. Next day he comes with his wife. A young, beautiful lady in a hat, carrying a baby girl in her arms. And plenty of baggage of all sorts. My Vasily Sergeich was spinning around her; couldn't take his eyes off her; couldn't praise her enough. 'Yes, brother Semyon, even in Siberia people can live!' . . . 'Well,' thinks I, 'just you wait; better not rejoice too soon.' . . . And from that time on, almost every week he went to Gyrino to find out if money had been sent from Russia. As for money—it took plenty! 'It's for my sake that her youth and beauty are going to ruin here in Siberia,' he says, 'sharing with me my bitter fate, and for this,' he says, 'I ought to provide her with every diversion.' To make it more cheerful for his lady he took up with officials and with all sorts of riff-raff. And there had to be food and drink for this crowd, of course, and they must have a piano, and a fuzzy little lap dog on the sofa—may it croak! . . . Luxury, in short, indulgence. The lady did not stay with him long. How could she? Clay, water, cold, no vegetables for you, no fruit; uneducated and drunken people all around, no manners at all, and she a pampered lady from the capital. . . . Naturally, she grew tired of it. Besides, her husband, say what you like, was no longer a gentleman, but an exile—not exactly an honor.

"Three years later, I remember, on the eve of the Assumption, someone shouted from the other side. I went over in the ferry, and what do I see but the lady—all muffled up, and with her a young gentleman, an official. There was a troika. . . . And after I ferried them across, they got in it and vanished into thin air! That was the last that was seen of them. Toward morning Vasily Sergeich galloped up to the ferry. 'Didn't my wife pass this way, Semyon, with a gentleman in spectacles?' . . . 'She did,' says I. 'Seek the wind in the fields!' He galloped off in pursuit of them, and didn't stop for five days and five nights. Afterwards, when I took him over to the other side, he threw himself down on the ferry, beat his head against the planks, and howled. 'So that's how it is,' says I. . . . I laughed and recalled to him: 'Even in Siberia people can live!' And he beat his head all the more.

"After that he began to long for freedom. His wife had slipped away to Russia, so, naturally, he was drawn there, both to see her and to rescue her from her lover. And, my friend, he took to galloping off every day, either to the post office or the authorities; he kept sending in petitions, and presenting them personally, asking to be pardoned so he could go back home; and he used to tell how he had spent some two hundred rubles on telegrams alone. He sold his land, and mortgaged his house to the Jews. He grew gray, stooped, and yellow in the face, as if he was consumptive. He'd talk to you and go: khe-khe-khe . . . and there would be tears in his eyes. He struggled with those petitions for eight years, but now he has recovered his spirits and is more cheerful: he's thought up a new indulgence. His daughter, you see, has grown up. He keeps an eye on her, dotes on her. And, to tell the truth, she's all right, a pretty little thing, black-browed, and with a lively disposition. Every Sunday he goes to church with her in Gyrino. Side by side they stand on the ferry, she laughing and he not taking his eyes off her. 'Yes, Semyon,' says he, 'even in Siberia people can live. Even in Siberia there is happiness. Look,' says he, 'see what a daughter I've got! I suppose you wouldn't find another like her if you went a thousand versts.' . . . 'Your daughter,' says I, 'is a fine young lady, that's true, certainly. . . .' But I think to myself: Wait a while. . . . The girl is young, her blood is dancing, she wants to live, and what life is there here? And, my friend, she did begin to fret. . . . She withered and withered, wasted away, fell ill; and now she's completely worn out. Consumption.

"That's your Siberian happiness for you, the pestilence take it! That's how people can live in Siberia! . . . He's taken to running after doctors and taking them home with him. As soon as he hears that there's a doctor or quack two or three hundred versts away, he goes to fetch him. A terrible lot of money has been spent on doctors; to my way of thinking, it would have been better to spend it on drink. . . . She'll die anyway. She's certain to die, and then he'll be completely lost. He'll hang himself from grief, or run away to Russia—that's sure. He'll run away, they'll catch him, there'll be a trial, and then hard labor; they'll give him a taste of the lash. . . ."

"Good, good," muttered the Tartar, shivering with cold.

"What's good?" asked Preacher.

"Wife and daughter. . . . Let hard labor, let suffer; he saw his wife and daughter. . . . You say: want nothing. But nothing is bad! Wife was with him three years—God gave him that. Nothing is bad; three years is good. How you not understand?"

Shivering and stuttering, straining to pick out the Russian words, of which he knew so few, the Tartar said God forbid one should fall sick and die in a strange land, and be buried in the cold, sodden earth; that if his wife came to him even for one day, even for one hour, he would be willing to accept any torture whatsoever, and thank God for it. Better one day of happiness than nothing.

After that he again described the beautiful and clever wife he had left at home; then, clutching his head with both hands, he began crying and assuring Semyon that he was innocent and had been falsely accused. His two brothers and his uncle stole some horses from a peasant, and beat the old man till he was half dead, and the commune had not judged fairly, but had contrived a sentence by which all three brothers were sent to Siberia, while the uncle, a rich man, remained at home.

"You'll get u-u-used to it!" said Semyon.

The Tartar relapsed into silence and fixed his tearful eyes on the fire; his face expressed bewilderment and fright, as though he still did not understand why he was here in the dark, in the damp, among strangers, instead of in the province of Simbirsk. Preacher lay down near the fire, chuckled at something, and began singing in an undertone.

"What joy has she with her father?" he said a little later. "He loves her, she's a consolation to him, it's true; but you have to mind your p's and q's with him, brother: he's a strict old man, a severe old man. And strictness is not what young girls want. . . . They want petting and ha-ha-ha and ho-ho-ho, scents and pomades! Yes. . . . Ekh, life, life!" sighed Semyon, getting up with difficulty. "The vodka's all gone, so it's time to sleep. Eh? I'm going, my boy."

Left alone, the Tartar put more brushwood onto the fire, lay down, and, looking into the blaze, began thinking of his native village, and of his wife: if she would come only for a month, even for a day, then, if she liked, she might go back again. Better a month or even a day than nothing. But if she kept her promise and came, how could he provide for her? Where could she live?

"If not something to eat, how you live?" the Tartar asked aloud.

He was paid only ten kopecks for working at the oars a day and a night; the passengers gave him tips, it was true, but the ferrymen shared everything among themselves, giving nothing to the Tartar, but only making fun of him. And he was hungry, cold, and frightened from want. . . . Now, when his whole body was shivering and aching, he ought to go into the hut and lie down to sleep, but he had nothing there to cover himself with, and it was colder there than on the river bank; here, too, he had nothing to put over him, but at least he could make a fire. . . .

In another week, when the floods had subsided and the ferry could sail, none of the ferrymen except Semyon would be needed, and the Tartar would begin going from village to village, looking for work and begging alms. His wife was only seventeen years old; beautiful, pampered, shy—could she possibly go from village to village, her face unveiled, begging? No, even to think of it was dreadful. . . .

It was already growing light; the barge, the bushes of rose willow, and the ripples on the water were clearly distinguishable, and looking back there was the steep clay precipice, below it the little hut thatched with brown straw, and above clung the huts of the villagers. The cocks were already crowing in the village.

The red clay precipice, the barge, the river, the strange, unkind people, hunger, cold, illness—perhaps all this did not exist in reality. Probably it was all a dream, thought the Tartar. He felt that he was asleep, and hearing his own snoring. . . .

Of course, he was at home in the province of Simbirsk, and he had only to call his wife by name for her to answer, and in the next room his mother. . . . However, what awful dreams there are! Why? The Tartar smiled and opened his eyes. What river was this? The Volga?

It was snowing.

"Bo-o-at!" someone shouted from the other side. "Kar-ba-a-s!"

The Tartar woke up and went to wake his comrades, to row over to the other side. Putting on their torn sheepskins as they came, the ferrymen appeared on the bank, swearing in hoarse, sleepy voices, and shivering from the cold. After their sleep, the river, from which there came a piercing gust of cold air, evidently struck them as revolting and sinister. They were not quick to jump into the barge. The Tartar and the three ferry-men took up the long, broad-bladed oars, which looked like crabs' claws in the darkness. Semyon leaned his belly against the long tiller. The shouting from the other side continued, and two shots were fired from a revolver; the man probably thought that the ferrymen were asleep or had gone off to the village tavern.

"All right, plenty of time!" said Preacher in the tone of a man who is convinced that there is no need to hurry in this world—that it makes no difference, really, and nothing will come of it.

The heavy, clumsy barge drew away from the bank and floated between the rose willows; and only because the willows slowly receded was it possible to see that the barge was not standing still but moving. The ferrymen plied the oars evenly, in unison; Preacher hung over the tiller on his belly, and, describing an arc in the air, flew from one side of the boat to the other. In the darkness it looked as if the men were sitting on some antediluvian animal with long paws, and sailing to a cold, bleak land, the very one of which we sometimes dream in nightmares.

They passed beyond the willows and floated out into the open. The rhythmic thump and splash of the oars was now audible on the further shore, and someone shouted, "Hurry! Hurry!" Another ten minutes passed, and the barge bumped heavily against the landing stage.

"And it keeps coming down, and coming down!" muttered Semyon, wiping the snow from his face. "Where it comes from, God only knows!"

On the other side stood a thin old man of medium height wearing a jacket lined with fox fur and a white lambskin cap. He was standing at a little distance from his horses and not moving; he had a concentrated, morose expression, as if, trying to remember something, he had grown angry with his unyielding memory. When Semyon went up to him with a smile and took off his cap, he said, "I'm hastening to Anastasyevka. My daughter is worse again, and they say there's a new doctor at Anastasyevka."

They dragged the tarantass onto the barge and rowed back. The man, whom Semyon called Vasily Sergeich, stood motionless all the way back, his thick lips tightly compressed, his eyes fixed on one spot; when the coachman asked permission to smoke in his presence, he made no reply, as if he had not heard. And Semyon, hanging over the tiller on his belly, glanced mockingly at him and said, "Even in Siberia people can live. Li-i-ve!"

There was a triumphant expression on Preacher's face, as if he had proved something and was rejoicing that it had turned out exactly as he had surmised. The helpless, unhappy look of the man in the fox-lined jacket evidently afforded him great satisfaction.

"It's muddy driving now, Vasily Sergeich," he said when

the horses were harnessed on the bank. "You'd better have waited a week or two till it gets drier. . . . Or else not have gone at all. . . . If there were any sense in going, but, as you yourself know, people have been driving about for ever and ever, by day and by night, and there's never any sense in it. That's the truth!"

Vasily Sergeich tipped him without a word, got into the tarantass, and drove off.

"See there, he's gone galloping off for a doctor!" said Semyon, shrinking with cold. "Yes, looking for a real doctor is like chasing the wind in the fields, or catching the devil by the tail, damn your soul! What freaks! Lord forgive me, a sinner!"

The Tartar went up to Preacher and, looking at him with hatred and abhorrence, trembling, mixing Tartar words with his broken Russian, said, "He is good—good. You bad! You bad! Gentleman is good soul, excellent, and you beast, you bad! Gentleman alive and you dead. . . . God created man to live, be joyful, be sad and sorrow, but you want nothing. . . . You not live, you stone, clay! Stone want nothing and you want nothing. . . . You stone—and God not love you, love gentleman!"

Everyone laughed; the Tartar frowned scornfully and, with a gesture of despair, wrapped himself in his rags and went to the fire. Semyon and the ferrymen trailed off to the hut.

"It's cold," said one of the ferrymen hoarsely as he stretched out on the straw that covered the damp floor.

"Well, it's not warm!" one of the others agreed. "It's a hard life!"

They all lay down. The door was blown open by the wind, and snow drifted into the hut. No one felt like getting up and closing the door; it was cold and they were lazy.

"I'm all right!" said Semyon, falling asleep. "God give everyone such a life."

"You're a hard case, we know that. Even the devils won't take you!"

From outside there came sounds like the howling of a dog.

"What's that? Who's there?"

"It's the Tartar crying."

"Crying? He's a funny one."

"He'll get u-u-used to it!" said Semyon, and instantly fell asleep.

Soon the others fell asleep too. And the door remained unclosed.

Interpretive Questions

1. Is Chekhov suggesting that Semyon has made a successful adjustment to living in exile or that he has become subhuman?
2. Why does Semyon say that the longing for wife, family, and freedom comes from the devil?
3. Why is the Tartar the only exile in the story who has been sentenced to Siberia unjustly?
4. Was Vasily Sergeich right to establish a home with his family in Siberia, according to Chekhov?
5. Does Chekhov think freedom in Siberia is no freedom at all?

VI

The political theory expressed in the Declaration of Independence is part of a long philosophical tradition. Selections from three of the works central to this tradition appear earlier in this Series: Aristotle's Politics, *Hobbe's* Leviathan, *and Locke's* Second Treatise of Government. *Each discusses the purpose of government. Aristotle holds that the aim of the state is to provide first necessities and then those things that contribute to the good life. Hobbes claims that the state brings order and security to human associations. And Locke says that the state is formed to preserve lives, liberties, and possessions of individuals.*

Each of these theories of government is based on a particular view of human nature. Aristotle sees human beings as social by nature: the state is the natural development of the human desire to form associations. According to Hobbes, human beings are naturally aggressive and selfish: the creation of a powerful state is the only way to keep individuals from attacking and abusing one another. Locke maintains that human beings by nature have certain rights and are subject to universal moral laws: governments are formed to make sure that these rights are respected and that moral laws are observed. What view of human nature underlies the Declaration, and how does this view compare with those of Politics, Of Commonwealth, *and* Of Civil Government?

The Declaration of Independence

In Congress, July 4, 1776
The unanimous Declaration of the thirteen United States of America

When in the course of human events, it becomes necessary for one people to dissolve the political bands which have connected them with another, and to assume among the powers of the earth, the separate and equal station to which the Laws of Nature and of Nature's God entitle them, a decent respect to the opinions of mankind requires that they should declare the causes which impel them to the separation.

We hold these truths to be self-evident, that all men are created equal, that they are endowed by their Creator with certain unalienable rights, that among these are life, liberty and the pursuit of happiness. That to secure these rights, governments are instituted among men, deriving their just powers from the consent of the governed. That whenever any form of government becomes destructive of these ends, it is the right of the people to alter or to abolish it, and to institute new government, laying its foundation on such principles and organizing its powers in such form, as to them shall seem most likely to effect their safety and happiness. Prudence, indeed, will dictate that governments long established should not be changed for light and transient causes; and accordingly all experience hath shown, that mankind are more disposed to suffer, while evils are sufferable, than to right themselves by abolishing the forms to which they are accustomed. But when a long train of abuses and usurpations, pursuing invariably the same object evinces a design to reduce them under absolute despotism, it is their right, it is their duty, to throw off such government, and to provide new guards for their future security. Such has been the patient sufferance of these Colonies; and such is now the necessity which constrains them to alter their former systems of government. The history of the present King of Great Britain is a history of repeated injuries and usurpations, all having in direct object the establishment of an absolute tyranny over these States. To prove this, let facts be submitted to a candid world.

He has refused his assent to laws, the most wholesome and necessary for the public good.

He has forbidden his Governors to pass laws of immediate and pressing importance, unless suspended in their operation till his assent should be obtained; and when so suspended, he has utterly neglected to attend to them.

He has refused to pass other laws for the accommodation of large districts of people, unless those people would relinquish the right of representation in the Legislature, a right inestimable to them and formidable to tyrants only.

He has called together legislative bodies at places unusual, uncomfortable, and distant from the depository of their public records, for the sole purpose of fatiguing them into compliance with his measures.

He has dissolved representative houses repeatedly, for opposing with manly firmness his invasions on the rights of the people.

He has refused for a long time, after such dissolutions, to cause others to be elected; whereby the legislative powers, incapable of annihilation, have returned to the people at large for their exercise; the State remaining in the meantime exposed to all the dangers of invasion from without and convulsions within.

He has endeavored to prevent the population of these states; for that purpose obstructing the laws of naturalization of foreigners; refusing to pass others to encourage their migration hither, and raising the conditions of new appropriations of lands.

He has obstructed the administration of justice, by refusing his assent to laws for establishing judiciary powers.

He has made judges dependent on his will alone, for the tenure of their offices, and the amount and payment of their salaries.

He has erected a multitude of new offices, and sent hither swarms of officers to harass our people, and eat out their substance.

He has kept among us, in times of peace, standing armies without the consent of our legislatures.

He has affected to render the military independent of and superior to the civil power.

He has combined with others to subject us to a jurisdiction foreign to our constitution, and unacknowledged by our laws; giving his assent to their acts of pretended legislation:

For quartering large bodies of armed troops among us:

For protecting them, by a mock trial, from punishment for any murders which they should commit on the inhabitants of these States:

For cutting off our trade with all parts of the world:

For imposing taxes on us without our consent:

For depriving us in many cases, of the benefits of trial by jury:

For transporting us beyond seas to be tried for pretended offenses:

For abolishing the free system of English laws in a neighboring Province, establishing therein an arbitrary government, and enlarging its boundaries so as to render it at once an example and fit instrument for introducing the same absolute rule into these Colonies:

For taking away our Charters, abolishing our most valuable laws, and altering fundamentally the forms of our governments:

For suspending our own Legislatures, and declaring themselves invested with power to legislate for us in all cases whatsoever.

He has abdicated government here, by declaring us out of his protection and waging war against us.

He has plundered our seas, ravaged our coasts, burnt our towns, and destroyed the lives of our people.

He is at this time transporting large armies of foreign mercenaries to complete the works of death, desolation and tyranny, already begun with circumstances of cruelty and perfidy scarcely paralleled in the most barbarous ages, and totally unworthy the head of a civilized nation.

He has constrained our fellow citizens taken captive on the high seas to bear arms against their country, to become the executioners of their friends and brethren, or to fall themselves by their hands.

He has excited domestic insurrections amongst us, and has endeavored to bring on the inhabitants of our frontiers, the merciless Indian savages, whose known rule of warfare, is an undistinguished destruction of all ages, sexes, and conditions.

In every stage of these oppressions we have petitioned for redress in the most humble terms: our repeated petitions have been answered only by repeated injury. A prince whose character is thus marked by every act which may define a tyrant is unfit to be the ruler of a free people.

Nor have we been wanting in attention to our British brethren. We have warned them from time to time of attempts by their legislature to extend an unwarrantable jurisdiction over us. We have reminded them of the circumstances of our emigration and settlement here. We have appealed to their native justice and magnanimity, and we have conjured them by the ties of our common kindred to disavow these usurpations, which would inevitably interrupt our connections and correspondence. They too have been deaf to the voice of justice and of consanguinity. We must, therefore, acquiesce in the necessity, which denounces our separation, and hold them, as we hold the rest of mankind, enemies in war, in peace friends.

WE, THEREFORE, the Representatives of the UNITED STATES OF AMERICA, in General Congress assembled, appealing to the Supreme Judge of the world for the rectitude of our intentions, do, in the name, and by authority of the good people of these Colonies, solemnly publish and declare, That these United Colonies are, and of right ought to be FREE and INDEPENDENT STATES; that they are absolved from all allegiance to the British Crown, and that all political connection between them and the State of Great Britain, is and ought to be totally dissolved; and that as Free and Independent States, they have full power to levy war, conclude peace, contract alliances, establish commerce, and to do all other acts and things which Independent States may of right do. And for the support of this declaration, with a firm reliance on the protection of Divine Providence, we mutually pledge to each other our lives, our fortunes, and our sacred honor.

JOHN HANCOCK.

New Hampshire
JOSIAH BARTLETT,
WM. WHIPPLE,
MATTHEW THORNTON.

Massachusetts Bay
SAML. ADAMS,
JOHN ADAMS,
ROBT. TREAT PAINE,
ELBRIDGE GERRY.

Rhode Island
STEP. HOPKINS,
WILLIAM ELLERY.

Connecticut
ROGER SHERMAN,
SAM'EL HUNTINGTON,
WM. WILLIAMS,
OLIVER WOLCOTT.

Georgia
BUTTON GWINNETT,
LYMAN HALL,
GEO. WALTON.

Maryland
SAMUEL CHASE,
WM. PACA,
THOS. STONE,
CHARLES CARROLL of Carrollton.

Virginia
GEORGE WYTHE,
RICHARD HENRY LEE,
TH. JEFFERSON,
BENJA. HARRISON,
THS. NELSON, JR.,
FRANCIS LIGHTFOOT LEE,
CARTER BRAXTON.

New York
WM. FLOYD,
PHIL. LIVINGSTON,
FRANS. LEWIS,
LEWIS MORRIS.

Pennsylvania
ROBT. MORRIS,
BENJAMIN RUSH,
BENJA. FRANKLIN,
JOHN MORTON,
GEO. CLYMER,
JAS. SMITH,
GEO. TAYLOR,
JAMES WILSON,
GEO. ROSS.

Delaware
CAESAR RODNEY,
GEO. READ,
THO. M'KEAN.

North Carolina
WM. HOOPER,
JOSEPH HEWES,
JOHN PENN.

South Carolina
EDWARD RUTLEDGE,
THOS. HEYWARD, JUNR.,
THOMAS LYNCH, JUNR.,
ARTHUR MIDDLETON.

New Jersey
RICHD. STOCKTON,
JNO. WITHERSPOON,
FRAS. HOPKINSON,
JOHN HART,
ABRA. CLARK.

Interpretive Questions

1. Does the argument for declaring independence depend on belief in God?

2. Could consent of the governed make any power of government just?

3. Are all the listed grievances violations of unalienable rights?

4. Why do the writers appeal to the Laws of Nature as well as to the Laws of Nature's God in justifying their break with Great Britain?

5. Is the right to overthrow the government an unalienable right?

Interpretation

Interpretation is the effort we make to understand what we read—to explain what an author's language is designed to make us think or feel. Interpreting the selections in this series requires effort because they have been written by keen thinkers. What these authors have to say cannot be taken in hastily. They use words carefully and precisely, but sometimes their language is difficult.

We begin to interpret a selection the first time we read it. It is helpful to make notes on what we understand and what puzzles us during this reading. Reading slowly is also important. Whenever you don't understand a passage, try pausing and rereading it. If an unfamiliar word stops you, look it up in a dictionary. If the author has used an ordinary word in an unfamiliar way, try to figure out its meaning in the context of the words or sentences surrounding it. If the passage is still unclear, make a note of it and move on; the meaning may be clarified later in the selection.

By the end of your first reading you may have only a glimmer of the selection's meaning, but your bits and pieces of understanding will help you on a second reading. This time you will be able to think about the selection as a whole, not just about the next step in an argument or how a story will end. You will be in a better position to consider why an author made a particular statement, why it was phrased in a certain way, and why it appears where it does in the selection. You should at least be able to pinpoint why you don't understand what the author is saying. During this reading, make a note of connections you find between different parts of the selection. Check the meaning of what you think you understand by expressing it in your own words.

Discussion is the last step in the interpretive process. It is an opportunity to compare your understanding of a selection's meaning with the interpretations of others, to discover significant passages that you may have overlooked, and to hear explanations of what you didn't understand. Occasionally discussion may provide your first inkling about a selection's meaning, but more often it explores ideas you had while reading. ■

VII

By and About Isaiah Berlin

(b. 1909)

Isaiah Berlin is best known for his writing on the history of ideas and political theory. In Berlin's view, the disciplines of history and philosophy are similar—and unlike the natural sciences. Scientists seek to isolate facts in order to deduce constant patterns; historians need to recognize the unique manner in which facts combine in concrete situations. He says that the search for governing laws is inappropriate in the field of history:

> Claims have been made . . . to be able to trace a structure of history . . . to discover the one and only true pattern into which alone all facts will be found to fit. But this is not, and can never be, accepted by any serious historian who wishes to establish the truth. . . . The same facts can be arranged in many patterns, seen from many perspectives, displayed in many lights, all of them equally valid. . . . Yet through it all the facts themselves will remain relatively "hard."

Berlin believes that the philosopher, like the historian, must recognize that he cannot be divorced from moral issues, although "it is not his business to preach or exhort or praise or condemn, only to illuminate." The philosopher's task is to

> explain what are the issues and values that are involved, to examine, and adjudicate between, the arguments for and against various conclusions, to make clear the forms of life which have come into collision, the ends of life, and perhaps the costs, which he has to decide between. In the end, of course, a man has to accept personal responsibility, and do what he thinks is right: his choice will be rational if he realizes the principles on which it is made, and free if he could have chosen otherwise. Such choices can be very agonizing. Obeying orders without reflection is easier.

The Declaration of Independence proclaims it a self-evident truth that "all men are created equal." This ideal of social equality is widely held today, but those who hold it do not always have a clear notion of what equality means. It is not so evident in what sense human beings are created equal: they obviously have widely differing mental and physical gifts. Nor is it evident in what ways human beings should be equal in a society: in every respect? in their standing before the law? in having opportunities to fulfill their desires? Berlin's analysis of equality and its relation to other values can help us clarify our own thinking about this important and complex notion.

Equality

Isaiah Berlin

In its simplest form the ideal of complete social equality embodies the wish that everything and everybody should be as similar as possible to everything and everybody else. It may serve to make this concept clearer if we try to conceive of some of the characteristics of a world in which no type of egalitarian would have anything to complain of. I doubt whether anyone has ever seriously desired to bring such a society into being, or even supposed such a society to be capable of being created. Nevertheless, it seems to me the demands for human equality which have been expressed both by philosophers and by men of action who have advocated or attempted the reform of society can best be represented as modifications of this absolute and perhaps absurd ideal. In the ideal egalitarian society, inequality—and this must ultimately mean dissimilarity—would be reduced to a minimum. The greatest single cause of complaint has been disparity in the possession, or enjoyment, of charac-

*A selection from *Concepts and Categories*.

teristics or commodities which have been strongly desired by men at most times—such as property, political or social power, status, opportunities for the development of faculties or the obtaining of experiences, social and personal liberties and privileges of all kinds. And the attack has taken the form of maintaining that a society in which some men are much richer or stronger or freer than others; in which some men possess the power of acquiring what they want and of preventing others from acquiring these same things or other things which they in turn want; or in which some men are paid homage and deferred to and permitted to live as they wish in ways and degrees which set them off from other men; all these are societies which offend either against the principle of natural rights, which according to those who hold this principle belong to all men as such; or against some rational principle whereby these differences may indeed be justified, but only by the provision of sufficient reasons for instituting or maintaining them. Disputes occur about what these rights are; or what reasons are sufficient or good; and whether such characteristics as differences of birth or of color or of religion or of wealth are true sources of unequal rights, or furnish good reasons for instituting political or social or other similar inequalities. There is, of course, a significant difference between those two ways of approach. Those who believe in natural rights differ mainly in establishing what these rights are, how their existence can be verified, whether all of them belong to all men, or only some to all, or only some to some; and whether equality is desirable in fields other than those covered by the claims created by the existence of natural rights. The other school—those who appeal to reason (though historically their views have overlapped with and become inextricably mingled with those of the believers in natural rights)—if they are to be consistent, must believe that equality should stretch over the entire field of human relations, and be modified only when there is sufficient reason to do so. Then disagreement may arise as to what constitutes a sufficient reason, and how great a modification a given reason justifies, and so forth. The first school, if it is consistent, will not object to inequalities, providing these do not infringe natural rights. But the second must protest against any inequality, unless a sufficient reason for it is produced. It is the latter, therefore, who go further, and are nearer to the extreme ideal which I should now like briefly to mention. Apart from the crucial question of what are and what are not sufficient reasons in such cases, it seems plain that inequalities of wealth or power are merely some among the possible inequalities which can excite opposition; they tend to be so prominent because they matter—affect human lives—more deeply, as things are, than other forms of inequality. But this is not always necessarily so. Even the most convinced social egalitarian does not normally object to the authority wielded by, let us say, the conductor of an orchestra. Yet there is no obvious reason why he should not. And there have been occasions—few and far between—when this has actually happened. Those who maintain that equality is the paramount good may not wish to be fobbed off with the explanation that the purpose of orchestral playing will not be served if every player is allowed equal authority with the conductor in deciding what is to be done. Inequality in the organization of an orchestra there patently is; the reason for it is the purpose of orchestral playing—the production of certain sounds in certain ways which cannot, in fact, be achieved without a measure of discipline which itself entails some degree of inequality in the distribution of authority. But a fanatical egalitarian could maintain that the inequality of the players in relation to the conductor is a greater evil than a poor performance of a symphonic work, and that it is better that no symphonic music be played at all if a conductorless orchestra is not feasible, than that such an institution should be allowed to offend against the principle of equality. To be more serious, the unequal distribution of natural gifts is a well-known obstacle to economic equality: in societies where there is a high degree of equality of economic opportunity, the strong and able and ambitious and cunning are likely to acquire more wealth or more power than those who lack these qualities. The fanatical egalitarian will look on this with horror; and because differences of natural talent will always tend towards the creation of inequalities, if only of prestige or influence, he will consequently wish—if equality is the paramount goal—to root out the evil at the source. He will tend to wish so to condition human beings that the highest degree of equality of natural properties is achieved, the greatest degree of mental and physical, that is to say total, uniformity—which alone will effectively preserve society, as far as possible, from the growth of inequalities of whatever kind. Only in a society where the greatest degree of similarity between the members occurs—where physical characteristics, mental endowment, emotional disposition, and conduct are as uniform as possible—where people differ as little as possible from each other in any respect whatever, will true equality be attainable. Only in such a society will it be possible to reduce to a minimum those differences of treatment, or of power, or of position, or of natural or acquired characteristics, that are liable to lead people to complain that they have not what others have, and to ask for reasons why this should be so. It may be that the creation of so uniform a society, whether or not it is intrinsically desirable, may not, in fact, be feasible. It may also be that even the attempt to approach it as closely as is humanly possible requires a degree of radical reorganization which cannot be carried out without a highly centralized and despotic authority—itself the cause of the maximum of inequality. Some convinced egalitarians have, as everyone knows, in practice accepted this as unavoidable, and have defended the institution of violent inequalities and the total suppression of many normal human claims as a necessary prerequisite for the creation of an ultimate equality. The moral and practical value of this is not relevant to the issue before us. What seems worth emphasizing is that so long as there are differences between men, some degree of inequality may occur; and that there is no kind of inequality against which, in principle, a pure egalitarian may not be moved to protest, simply on the ground that he sees no reason for tolerating it, no argument which seems to him more powerful than the argument for equality itself—equality which he regards not merely as an end in itself, but as *the* end, the principal goal of human life. I do not suppose that extreme equality of this type—the maximum similarity of a body of all but indiscernible human beings—has ever been consciously put forward as an ideal by any serious thinker. But if we ask what kinds of equality have in fact been demanded, we shall see, I think, that they are specific modifications of this absolute ideal, and that it therefore possesses the central importance of an ideal limit or idealized model at the heart of all egalitarian thought.

To examine some of these modifications. There are those who believe that natural human characteristics either cannot or should not be altered and that all that is necessary is equality of political and juridical rights. Provided that there exists equality before the law, such normal democratic principles as that of one man, one vote, some form of government arrived at by consent (actual or understood) between the members of the society, or at any rate the majority of them, and finally, a certain minimum of liberties—commonly called civil liberties—deemed necessary in order to enable men freely to exercise the legal and political rights entailed by this degree of equality, then, according to this view, no interference in other regions of activity (say, the economic) should be permitted. This is a common liberal doctrine of the last century. If it is complained that in a society where a large degree of political and legal equality is ensured, the strong and the clever and the ambitious may succeed in enriching themselves, or acquiring political power, "at the expense of"—that is to say, in such a way as to keep these goods from—other members of the society, and that this leads to patent inequalities, liberals of this school reply that this is the price for ensuring political and legal equality, and that the only method of preventing economic or social inequalities is by reducing the degree of political liberty or legal equality between men. This amounts to an admission that we must choose one of several ways of treating men as counting for only one; that they can be "counted for one" only in some respects, but not in others. For we are told, with considerable empirical evidence, that to count men for one and only one in every respect whatever is impracticable, that the full degree of, let us say, legal and political equality often results in economic and other forms of inequality, given the different endowments of men, and that only in an absolutely uniform, robot-like society, which no one wants, can this be effectively prevented. Those who believe this commonly maintain that the only inequality which should be avoided is an inequality based on characteristics which the individual cannot alter—unequal treatment based, for instance, on birth, or color, which human beings cannot alter at will. Given that all human beings start off with equal rights to acquire and hold property, to associate with each other in whatever ways they wish, to say whatever they will, and all the other traditional objectives of liberalism, and with no special rights or privileges attached to birth, color, and other physically unalterable characteristics, then even though some human beings, by skill or luck or natural endowment, do manage to acquire property or power of ascendancy which enables them to control the lives of others, or to acquire objects which the others are not in a position to acquire, then, since there is nothing in the constitution of the society that actually forbids such acquisitiveness, the principle of equality has not been infringed. This is a pure form of *laissez-faire* society which its proponents freely admit may lead to inequalities, but defend upon the ground that it gives an equal opportunity to all, a career genuinely open to all the talents—whereas any attempt to secure a greater degree of ultimate equality can only be obtained by interfering with this initial equalization of opportunity for all. In effect this is, of course, tantamount to a plea for liberty at the expense of total equality; for it is only pure anarchists who believe that the maximum degree of liberty is wholly compatible with the maximum degree of equality in all important respects, and are called mistaken or Utopian to the degree to which this proposition has in fact been falsified by experience. . . .

Equality is one value among many: the degree to which it is compatible with other ends depends on the concrete situation, and cannot be deduced from general laws of any kind; it is neither more nor less rational than any other ultimate principle; indeed it is difficult to see what is meant by considering it either rational or nonrational.

Yet the principle that every man shall count for one and no more than one demands a little more consideration before we finally abandon it as one of the ends pursued by men, needing neither explanation nor justification, being itself that which explains other rules or ethical principles. It seems . . . intimately bound up with the belief in general rules of conduct. This belief may rest upon religious or metaphysical or utilitarian grounds, or derive from the love of order or system as such.

However that may be, it often takes the form of a demand for fairness. The notions of equality and fairness are closely bound up: if, as a result of breaking a rule, a man derives benefits which he can obtain only so long as other men do not break but keep the rule, then no matter what other needs are being served by such a breach, the result is an offence against a principle best described as that of fairness, which is a form of desire for equality for its own sake. If I enter a bus and do not pay for my ticket, and conceal this fact from the conductor and the other passengers, and give the sum withheld to a pauper whose situation is thereby improved materially, it may be argued that at any rate from a utilitarian point of view I have done what is right. The bus company will not know of its loss; nor would so small a loss noticeably decrease "its" happiness; I possess a strong will and shall not fall into bad habits; the conductor has not noticed that he was not paid, and will not even so much as suffer from a sense of failure to carry out his duties; the passengers in their ignorance will not be led into temptation and demoralization, nor will there ensue any weakening of confidence between the persons concerned in the transaction, leading in the end to the discontinuance of the bus service. The general sum of happiness—in this case via that of the subsidized pauper—will surely have gone up to a greater degree than if I had paid my fare to the bus conductor. Nevertheless, quite apart from the morally relevant fact that, having entered into a quasi-contractual obligation to pay, I have broken my promise, my act would be condemned as unfair, for it would rightly be maintained that I can only gain advantage (or the pauper can only gain advantage) so long as the other passengers continue to behave as they did before—since if my act were generally followed no one would pay, and the buses would stop running. So long as my advantage directly depends on the fact that others continue to obey the rule which applies to me as much as to them, so that I alone profit by the exception which I have made in my own favor, such a relaxation of the rule for my benefit would be rightly stigmatized as unfair (as well as dishonest); and although critical situations can be easily imagined in which it would be morally better that I should act in this way and break my contract, or cheat, yet it is clear that a person of normal moral sensitiveness would cheat in this manner only with considerable qualms—qualms derived not merely from the fact that he has broken a contract, but from the sense of the unfairness of what he was doing. Indeed liability to such qualms is among the very criteria of what we call moral sensitiveness. If, despite them, a man resolved to commit such an act, his moral justification would necessarily take the form of invoking, and attempting to balance the claims of, ends or values other than those of equality. He would be drawn in one direction by such considerations as the sanctity of promises; the social need to keep one's word and preserve the rule of law and the social order; the intrinsic desirability of avoiding unfairness; and so on. These factors he would have to weigh against such others as the desirability of increasing happiness (in the case of the pauper) or of avoiding the creation of misery; the claims, say, of scientific curiosity; the desire to follow some romantic impulse or vision of life, and so on. And the same kinds of considerations will apply when exceptions are made to rules for "good" or "sufficient" reasons. The goodness of the reasons will depend upon the degree of value or importance attached to the purposes of motives adduced in justifying the exceptions, and these will vary as the moral convictions—the general outlooks—of different individuals or societies vary. I may consider it right to reward ability and achievement, and not, for example, honesty and kindness when they are accompanied by stupidity or ineptitude or failure. But others may well think this wrong, and the opposite morally right. I may think it right to reward the bearers of celebrated names or the descendants of famous families as such; or to deny certain rights to Negroes which I grant freely to Englishmen; and may try to defend this policy by maintaining that a society in which this is the normal practice seems to me intrinsically better, or more stable, or to accord more closely with some pattern sanctioned by my religion, or my metaphysical beliefs about the structure of the universe, or the laws of history; whereas you will reject a society dedicated to such practices as iniquitous because, let us assume, you reject my religion, or my metaphysics; or because you believe me to be interpreting them falsely, or think that a society constructed on such principles is intrinsically bad, or politically precarious; or simply because you believe so passionately in equality for its own sake that you are not deterred by the realization that the consequences which I (and perhaps you too) wish to avert may well be brought about by opposing my policies. There are many ways in which such basic disagreements can manifest themselves: one man or sect or political party may desire equality in one sphere of life, say in social or in legal relationships or legal status, and ignore the economic consequences; another may regard economic relationships as being supremely important, and be prepared to tolerate lack of social or legal equality for the sake of a given economic structure. Some may regard exceptions made in favor of specific gifts or genius as justifiable by social results. Others may regard this as unfair, but, in their turn, believe in some natural social hierarchy, like Burke,* and demand full equality of treatment upon each rung of the ladder—the only "true" equality—but bitterly oppose as being contrary to the natural order any at-

* *Burke.* Edmund Burke (1729-1797), British statesman and political thinker.

tempt to deny the existence or relevance of such rungs or hierarchies, with its accompaniment of demands for equal treatment for all. Consequently when, as often happens, a man admits that a law is administered fairly—that is to say with due regard to the principle of equality—but complains that the law itself is bad or iniquitous, we cannot always be clear about what is meant. The critic may wish to say that the more fairly the law in question is administered, the more this frustrates a principle of wider equality in which he himself believes, as when a law based upon the principle of discrimination between colored and white men is administered fairly, i.e. with scrupulous regard to equal treatment within each category, but is thereby itself the cause of inequality between colored and white men. But the critic may have other reasons for complaint. He may attack this law because it offends against some value other than equality—because it promotes misery, because it frustrates talent, because it makes for social instability, because it insists upon equality in what the attacker thinks unimportant matters, but ignores equality in what he regards as more important aspects of human life (the scale of importance being decided in terms of values other than equality itself); because it ignores the claims of a religion; because it fulfills the claims of religion; because it is obscure or vague or too difficult to obey; and for an infinity of other possible reasons—very commonly because, as in the instance given above, it permits one kind of equality at the expense of another, which can be a matter of fine nuance. . . .

Finally, those must not be forgotten who . . . object to all rules as such and desire a society, whether this is practicable or not, governed in an unsystematic manner by the will of an inspired leader, or by the unpredictable movement of the Volksgeist, or the "spirit" of a race, a party, a church. This amounts to rejection of rules, and of equality as an end valuable in itself, and it is as well to recognize that this attitude is not as rare or as ineffective as liberal and socialist thinkers have sometimes assumed. In its conflicts with the traditional Western principles of equality or justice or natural rights, or that minimum of civil liberties which is required to protect human beings from degradation and exploitation, romantic irrationalism has at times won easily enough. I cite this only as a warning against the thesis that the commandment to treat all men alike in like situations needs no independent argument to support it, and that the proper criteria for what constitutes likeness cannot be doubted or conflict with each other, but are something taken for granted by reasonable men, a form of the working of natural reason which needs no justification, but is as self-evident as the principle of identity or that red is different from green. This is far from being so; and the vicissitudes of liberal principles in the last, and especially this, century, seem partly due to the unwarranted assumption on the part of their defenders that those who reject these principles only do so through ignorance or intellectual indolence or mental perversity or blindness. Belief in equality—fairness—the view that unless there is a reason for it, recognized as sufficient by some identifiable criterion, one man should not be preferred to another, is a deep-rooted principle in human thought. It has been assimilated into many systems, those of the utilitarians and the theories of natural right, as well as various religious doctrines, but can be isolated from them, and has entered them less by way of logical connection, than by psychological affinity or because those who believed in these utilitarian or religious or metaphysical doctrines also in fact—perhaps from a craving for symmetry and unity that is at the root of all these views—believed in equality for its own sake, and therefore considered any society which did not make sufficient room for this principle to be to that degree worth less than one that did. In its extreme form egalitarianism requires the minimization of all differences between men, the obliteration of the maximum number of distinctions, the greatest possible degree of assimilation and uniformity to a single pattern. For all differences are capable of leading to irregularities of treatment. If this ideal is on the whole rejected in actual political doctrines, this seems mainly due to the fact that it conflicts with other ideals with which it cannot be wholly reconciled; indeed most ethical and political views are forms of less or more uneasy compromise between principles which in their extreme form cannot coexist. . . .

Interpretive Questions

1. Is affirmative action a form of inequality?
2. Are some kinds of inequality desirable?
3. Why does Berlin believe that freedom and equality may be opposed to each other?
4. Does Berlin think that full equality of treatment on each rung of the ladder is the only true equality?
5. Why does Berlin think the principle of equality is not self-evident?

VIII

By and About Isak Dinesen

(1885–1962)

Isak Dinesen is the pen name of Danish author Karen Blixen. Born Karen Christentze Dinesen, she became the Baroness von Blixen-Finecke in 1914, when she married her second cousin. She and her husband immigrated to the Kenya Colony in British East Africa and bought a coffee plantation near Nairobi. It was there that she began to write:

> After a time, I . . . gave up talking of the hard times or complaining about them, like a person in disgrace. But I . . . was young, and by instinct of self-preservation, I had to collect my energy on something, if I were not to be whirled away with the dust on the farm-roads, or the smoke on the plain. I began in the evenings to write stories, fairy-tales and romances, that would take my mind a long way off, to other countries and times.

Throughout her life, Dinesen was regarded as an unparalleled storyteller. This gift, she believed, linked her more closely to the culture of her adopted home:

> Fashions have changed, and the art of listening to a narrative has been lost in Europe. The Natives of Africa, who cannot read, have still got it; if you begin to them: "There was a man who walked out on the plain, and there he met another man," you have them all with you, their minds running upon the unknown track of the men on the plain. But white people, even if they feel that they ought to, cannot listen to a recital. If they do not become fidgety, and remember things that should be done at once, they fall asleep. The same people will ask you for something to read, and may then sit all through an evening absorbed in any kind of print handed them, they will even then read a speech. They have been accustomed to take in their impressions by the eye.

The depression of 1931 forced Dinesen to return to Denmark, bankrupt and in poor health. She lived and wrote in her childhood home until her death.

Sorrow-Acre

Isak Dinesen

The low, undulating Danish landscape was silent and serene, mysteriously wide-awake in the hour before sunrise. There was not a cloud in the pale sky, not a shadow along the dim, pearly fields, hills and woods. The mist was lifting from the valleys and hollows, the air was cool, the grass and the foliage dripping wet with morning-dew. Unwatched by the eyes of man, and undisturbed by his activity, the country breathed a timeless life, to which language was inadequate.

All the same, a human race had lived on this land for a thousand years, had been formed by its soil and weather, and had marked it with its thoughts, so that now no one could tell where the existence of the one ceased and the other began. The thin grey line of a road, winding across the plain and up and down hills, was the fixed materialisation of human longing, and of the human notion that it is better to be in one place than another.

A child of the country would read this open landscape like a book. The irregular mosaic of meadows and cornlands was a picture, in timid green and yellow, of the people's struggle for its daily bread; the centuries had taught it to plough and sow in this way. On a distant hill the immovable wings of a windmill, in a small blue cross against the sky, delineated a later stage in the career of bread. The blurred outline of thatched roofs—a low, brown growth of the earth—where the huts of the village thronged together, told the history, from his cradle to his grave, of the peasant, the creature nearest to the soil and dependent on it, prospering in a fertile year and dying in years of drought and pests.

A little higher up, with the faint horizontal line of the white cemetery-wall round it, and the vertical contour of tall poplars by its side, the red-tiled church bore witness, as far as the eye reached, that this was a Christian country. The child of the land knew it as a strange house, inhabited only for a few hours every seventh day, but with a strong, clear voice in it to give out the joys and sorrows of the land: a plain, square embodiment of the nation's trust in the justice and mercy of heaven. But where, amongst cupular woods and groves, the lordly, pyramidal silhouette of the cut lime avenues rose in the air, there a big country house lay.

The child of the land would read much within these elegant, geometrical ciphers on the hazy blue. They spoke of power, the lime trees paraded round a stronghold. Up here was decided the destiny of the surrounding land and of the men and beasts upon it, and the peasant lifted his eyes to the green pyramids with awe. They spoke of dignity, decorum and taste. Danish soil grew no finer flower than the mansion to which the long avenue led. In its lofty rooms life and death bore themselves with stately grace. The country house did not gaze upward, like the church, nor down to the ground like the huts;

it had a wider earthly horizon than they, and was related to much noble architecture all over Europe. Foreign artisans had been called in to panel and stucco it, and its own inhabitants travelled and brought back ideas, fashions and things of beauty. Paintings, tapestries, silver and glass from distant countries had been made to feel at home here, and now formed part of Danish country life.

The big house stood as firmly rooted in the soil of Denmark as the peasants' huts, and was as faithfully allied to her four winds and her changing seasons, to her animal life, trees and flowers. Only its interests lay in a higher plane. Within the domain of the lime trees it was no longer cows, goats and pigs on which the minds and the talk ran, but horses and dogs. The wild fauna, the game of the land, that the peasant shook his fist at, when he saw it on his young green rye or in his ripening wheat field, to the residents of the country houses were the main pursuit and the joy of existence.

The writing in the sky solemnly proclaimed continuance, a worldly immortality. The great country houses had held their ground through many generations. The families who lived in them revered the past as they honoured themselves, for the history of Denmark was their own history.

A Rosenkrantz had sat at Rosenholm, a Juel at Hverringe, a Skeel at Gammel-Estrup as long as people remembered. They had seen kings and schools of style succeed one another and, proudly and humbly, had made over their personal existence to that of their land, so that amongst their equals and with the peasants they passed by its name: Rosenholm, Hverringe, Gammel-Estrup. To the King and the country, to his family and to the individual lord of the manor himself it was a matter of minor consequence which particular Rosenkrantz, Juel or Skeel, out of a long row of fathers and sons, at the moment in his person incarnated the fields and woods, the peasants, cattle and game of the estate. Many duties rested on the shoulders of the big landowners—towards God in heaven, towards the King, his neighbour and himself—and they were all harmoniously consolidated into the idea of his duties towards his land. Highest amongst these ranked his obligation to uphold the sacred continuance, and to produce a new Rosenkrantz, Juel or Skeel for the service of Rosenholm, Hverringe and Gammel-Estrup.

Female grace was prized in the manors. Together with good hunting and fine wine it was the flower and emblem of the higher existence led there, and in many ways the families prided themselves more on their daughters than on their sons.

The ladies who promenaded in the lime avenues, or drove through them in heavy coaches with four horses, carried the future of the name in their laps and were, like dignified and debonair caryatides, holding up the houses. They were themselves conscious of their value, kept up their price, and moved in a sphere of pretty worship and self-worship. They might even be thought to add to it, on their own, a graceful, arch, paradoxical haughtiness. For how free were they, how powerful! Their lords might rule the country, and allow themselves many liberties, but when it came to that supreme matter of legitimacy which was the vital principle of their world, the centre of gravity lay with them.

The lime trees were in bloom. But in the early morning only a faint fragrance drifted through the garden, an airy message, an aromatic echo of the dreams during the short summer night.

In a long avenue that led from the house all the way to the end of the garden, where, from a small white pavilion in the classic style, there was a great view over the fields, a young man walked. He was plainly dressed in brown, with pretty linen and lace, bare-headed, with his hair tied by a ribbon. He was dark, a strong and sturdy figure with fine eyes and hands; he limped a little on one leg.

The big house at the top of the avenue, the garden and the fields had been his childhood's paradise. But he had travelled and lived out of Denmark, in Rome and Paris, and he was at present appointed to the Danish Legation to the Court of King George, the brother of the late, unfortunate young Danish Queen. He had not seen his ancestral home for nine years. It made him laugh to find, now, everything so much smaller than he remembered it, and at the same time he was strangely moved by meeting it again. Dead people came towards him and smiled at him; a small boy in a ruff ran past him with his hoop and kite, in passing gave him a clear glance and laughingly asked: "Do you mean to tell me that you are I?" He tried to catch him in the flight, and to answer him: "Yes, I assure you that I am you," but the light figure did not wait for a reply.

The young man, whose name was Adam, stood in a particular relation to the house and the land. For six months he had been heir to it all; nominally he was so even at this moment. It was this circumstance which had brought him from England, and on which his mind was dwelling, as he walked along slowly.

The old lord up at the manor, his father's brother, had had much misfortune in his domestic life. His wife had died young, and two of his children in infancy. The one son then left to him, his cousin's playmate, was a sickly and morose boy. For ten years the father travelled with him from one watering place to another, in Germany and Italy, hardly ever in other company than that of his silent, dying child, sheltering the faint flame of life with both hands, until such time as it could be passed over to a new bearer of the name. At the same time another misfortune had struck him: he fell into disfavour at Court, where till now he had held a fine position. He was about to rehabilitate his family's prestige through the marriage which he had arranged for his son, when before it could take place the bridegroom died, not yet twenty years old.

Adam learned of his cousin's death, and his own changed fortune, in England, through his ambitious and triumphant mother. He sat with her letter in his hand and did not know what to think about it.

If this, he reflected, had happened to him while he was still a boy, in Denmark, it would have meant all the world to him. It would be so now with his friends and schoolfellows, if they were in his place, and they would, at this moment, be congratulating or envying him. But he was neither covetous nor vain by nature; he had faith in his own talents and had been content to know that his success in life depended on his personal ability. His slight infirmity had always set him a little apart from other boys; it had, perhaps, given him a keener sensibility of many things in life, and he did not, now, deem it quite right that the head of the family should limp on one leg. He did not even see his prospects in the same light as his people at home. In England he had met with greater wealth and magnificence than they dreamed of; he had been in love with, and made happy by, an English lady of such rank and fortune that to her, he felt, the finest estate of Denmark would look but like a child's toy farm.

And in England, too, he had come in touch with the great new ideas of the age: of nature, of the right and freedom of man, of justice and beauty. The universe, through them, had become infinitely wider to him; he wanted to find out still more about it and was planning to travel to America, to the new world. For a moment he felt trapped and imprisoned, as if the dead people of his name, from the family vault at home, were stretching out their parched arms for him.

But at the same time he began to dream at night of the old

house and garden. He had walked in these avenues in dream, and had smelled the scent of the flowering limes. When at Ranelagh an old gypsy woman looked at his hand and told him that a son of his was to sit in the seat of his fathers, he felt a sudden, deep satisfaction, queer in a young man who till now had never given his sons a thought.

Then, six months later, his mother again wrote to tell him that his uncle had himself married the girl intended for his dead son. The head of the family was still in his best age, not over sixty, and although Adam remembered him as a small, slight man, he was a vigorous person; it was likely that his young wife would bear him sons.

Adam's mother in her disappointment lay the blame on him. If he had returned to Denmark, she told him, his uncle might have come to look upon him as a son, and would not have married; nay, he might have handed the bride over to him. Adam knew better. The family estate, differing from the neighbouring properties, had gone down from father to son ever since a man of their name first sat there. The tradition of direct succession was the pride of the clan and a sacred dogma to his uncle; he would surely call for a son of his own flesh and bone.

But at the news the young man was seized by a strange, deep, aching remorse towards his old home in Denmark. It was as if he had been making light of a friendly and generous gesture, and disloyal to someone unfailingly loyal to him. It would be just, he thought, if from now the place should disown and forget him. Nostalgia, which before he had never known, caught hold of him; for the first time he walked in the streets and parks of London as a stranger.

He wrote to his uncle and asked if he might come and stay with him, begged leave from the Legation and took ship for Denmark. He had come to the house to make his peace with it; he had slept little in the night, and was up so early and walking in the garden, to explain himself, and to be forgiven.

While he walked, the still garden slowly took up its day's work. A big snail, of the kind that his grandfather had brought back from France, and which he remembered eating in the house as a child, was already, with dignity, dragging a silver train down the avenue. The birds began to sing; in an old tree under which he stopped a number of them were worrying an owl; the rule of the night was over.

He stood at the end of the avenue and saw the sky lightening. An ecstatic clarity filled the world; in half an hour the sun would rise. A rye field here ran along the garden; two roe-deer were moving in it and looked roseate in the dawn. He gazed out over the fields, where as a small boy he had ridden his pony, and towards the wood where he had killed his first stag. He remembered the old servants who had taught him; some of them were now in their graves.

The ties which bound him to this place, he reflected, were of a mystic nature. He might never again come back to it, and it would make no difference. As long as a man of his own blood and name should sit in the house, hunt in the fields and be obeyed by the people in the huts, wherever he travelled on earth, in England or amongst the red Indians of America, he himself would still be safe, would still have a home, and would carry weight in the world.

His eyes rested on the church. In old days, before the time of Martin Luther, younger sons of great families, he knew, had entered the Church of Rome, and had given up individual wealth and happiness to serve the greater ideals. They, too, had bestowed honour upon their homes and were remembered in its registers. In the solitude of the morning half in jest he let his mind run as it listed; it seemed to him that he might speak to the land as to a person, as to the mother of his race.

"Is it only my body that you want," he asked her, "while you reject my imagination, energy and emotions? If the world might be brought to acknowledge that the virtue of our name does not belong to the past only, will it give you no satisfaction?" The landscape was so still that he could not tell whether it answered him yes or no.

After a while he walked on, and came to the new French rose garden laid out for the young mistress of the house. In England he had acquired a freer taste in gardening, and he wondered if he could liberate these blushing captives, and make them thrive outside their cut hedges. Perhaps, he meditated, the elegantly conventional garden would be a floral portrait of his young aunt from Court, whom he had not yet seen.

As once more he came to the pavilion at the end of the avenue his eyes were caught by a bouquet of delicate colours which could not possibly belong to the Danish summer morning. It was in fact his uncle himself, powdered and silk-stockinged, but still in a brocade dressing-gown, and obviously sunk in deep thought. "And what business, or what meditations," Adam asked himself, "drags a connoisseur of the beautiful, but three months married to a wife of seventeen, from his bed into his garden before sunrise?" He walked up to the small, slim, straight figure.

His uncle on his side showed no surprise at seeing him, but then he rarely seemed surprised at anything. He greeted him, with a compliment on his matutinality, as kindly as he had done on his arrival last evening. After a moment he looked to the sky, and solemnly proclaimed: "It will be a hot day." Adam, as a child, had often been impressed by the grand, ceremonial manner in which the old lord would state the common happenings of existence; it looked as if nothing had changed here, but all was what it used to be.

The uncle offered the nephew a pinch of snuff. "No, thank you, Uncle," said Adam, "it would ruin my nose to the scent of your garden, which is as fresh as the Garden of Eden, newly created." "From every tree of which," said his uncle, smiling, "thou, my Adam, mayest freely eat." They slowly walked up the avenue together.

The hidden sun was now already gilding the top of the tallest trees. Adam talked of the beauties of nature, and of the greatness of Nordic scenery, less marked by the hand of man than that of Italy. His uncle took the praise of the landscape as a personal compliment, and congratulated him because he had not, in likeness to many young travellers in foreign countries, learned to despise his native land. No, said Adam, he had lately in England longed for the fields and woods of his Danish home. And he had there become acquainted with a new piece of Danish poetry which had enchanted him more than any English or French work. He named the author, Johannes Ewald, and quoted a few of the mighty, turbulent verses.

"And I have wondered, while I read," he went on after a pause, still moved by the lines he himself had declaimed, "that we have not till now understood how much our Nordic mythology in moral greatness surpasses that of Greece and Rome. If it had not been for the physical beauty of the ancient gods, which has come down to us in marble, no modern mind could hold them worthy of worship. They were mean, capricious and treacherous. The gods of our Danish forefathers are as much more divine than they as the Druid is nobler than the Augur. For the fair gods of Asgaard did possess the sublime human virtues; they were righteous, trustworthy, benevolent and even, within a barbaric age, chivalrous." His uncle here for the first time appeared to take any real interest in the conversation. He stopped, his majestic nose a little in the air. "Ah, it was easier to them," he said.

"What do you mean, Uncle?" Adam asked. "It was a great deal easier," said his uncle, "to the northern gods than to those of Greece to be, as you will have it, righteous and benevolent. To my mind it even reveals a weakness in the souls of our ancient Danes that they should consent to adore such divinities." "My dear uncle," said Adam, smiling. "I have always felt that you would be familiar with the modes of Olympus. Now please let me share your insight, and tell me why virtue should come easier to our Danish gods than to those of milder climates." "They were not as powerful," said his uncle.

"And does power," Adam again asked, "stand in the way of virtue?" "Nay," said his uncle gravely. "Nay, power is in itself the supreme virtue. But the gods of which you speak were never all-powerful. They had, at all times, by their side those darker powers which they named the Jotuns, and who worked the suffering, the disasters, the ruin of our world. They might safely give themselves up to temperance and kindness. The omnipotent gods," he went on, "have no such facilitation. With their omnipotence they take over the woe of the universe."

They had walked up the avenue till they were in view of the house. The old lord stopped and ran his eyes over it. The stately building was the same as ever; behind the two tall front windows, Adam knew, was now his young aunt's room. His uncle turned and walked back.

"Chivalry," he said, "chivalry, of which you were speaking, is not a virtue of the omnipotent. It must needs imply mighty rival powers for the knight to defy. With a dragon inferior to him in strength, what figure will St. George cut? The knight who finds no superior forces ready to hand must invent them, and combat wind-mills; his knighthood itself stipulates dangers, vileness, darkness on all sides of him. Nay, believe me, my nephew, in spite of his moral worth, your chivalrous Odin of Asgaard as a Regent must take rank below that of Jove who avowed his sovereignty, and accepted the world which he ruled. But you are young," he added, "and the experience of the aged to you will sound pedantic."

He stood immovable for a moment and then with deep gravity proclaimed: "The sun is up."

The sun did indeed rise above the horizon. The wide landscape was suddenly animated by its splendour, and the dewy grass shone in a thousand gleams.

"I have listened to you, Uncle," said Adam, "with great interest. But while we have talked you yourself have seemed to me preoccupied; your eyes have rested on the field outside the garden, as if something of great moment, a matter of life and death, was going on there. Now that the sun is up, I see the mowers in the rye and hear them whetting their sickles. It is, I remember you telling me, the first day of the harvest. That is a great day to a landowner and enough to take his mind away from the gods. It is very fine weather, and I wish you a full barn."

The elder man stood still, his hands on his walking-stick. "There is indeed," he said at last, "something going on in that field, a matter of life and death. Come, let us sit down here, and I will tell you the whole story." They sat down on the seat that ran all along the pavilion, and while he spoke the old lord of the land did not take his eyes off the rye field.

"A week ago, on Thursday night," he said, "someone set fire to my barn at Rødmosegaard—you know the place, close to the moor—and burned it all down. For two or three days we could not lay hands on the offender. Then on Monday morning the keeper at Rødmose, with the wheelwright over there, came up to the house; they dragged with them a boy, Goske Piil, a widow's son, and they made their Bible oath that he had done it; they had themselves seen him sneaking round the barn by nightfall on Thursday. Goske had no good name on the farm; the keeper bore him a grudge upon an old matter of poaching, and the wheelwright did not like him either, for he did, I believe, suspect him with his young wife. The boy, when I talked to him, swore to his innocence, but he could not hold his own against the two old men. So I had him locked up, and meant to send him in to our judge of the district, with a letter.

"The judge is a fool, and would naturally do nothing but what he thought I wished him to do. He might have the boy sent to the convict prison for arson, or put amongst the soldiers as a bad character and a poacher. Or again, if he thought that that was what I wanted, he could let him off.

"I was out riding in the fields, looking at the corn that was soon ripe to be mowed, when a woman, the widow, Goske's mother, was brought up before me, and begged to speak to me. Anne-Marie is her name. You will remember her; she lives in the small house east of the village. She has not got a good name in the place either. They tell as a girl she had a child and did away with it.

"From five days' weeping her voice was so cracked that it was difficult for me to understand what she said. Her son, she told me at last, had indeed been over at Rødmose on Thursday, but for no ill purpose; he had gone to see someone. He was her only son, she called the Lord God to witness on his innocence, and she wrung her hands to me that I should save the boy for her.

"We were in the rye field that you and I are looking at now. That gave me an idea. I said to the widow: 'If in one day, between sunrise and sunset, with your own hands you can mow this field, and it be well done, I will let the case drop and you shall keep your son. But if you cannot do it, he must go, and it is not likely that you will then ever see him again.'

"She stood up then and gazed over the field. She kissed my riding boot in gratitude for the favour shown to her."

The old lord here made a pause, and Adam said: "Her son meant much to her?" "He is her only child," said his uncle. "He means to her her daily bread and support in old age. It may be said that she holds him as dear as her own life. As," he added, "within a higher order of life, a son to his father means the name and the race, and he holds him as dear as life everlasting. Yes, her son means much to her. For the mowing of that field is a day's work to three men, or three days' work to one man. Today, as the sun rose, she set to her task. And down there, by the end of the field, you will see her now, in a blue head-cloth, with the man I have set to follow her and to ascertain that she does the work unassisted, and with two or three friends by her, who are comforting her."

Adam looked down, and did indeed see a woman in a blue head-cloth, and a few other figures in the corn.

They sat for a while in silence. "Do you yourself," Adam then said, "believe the boy to be innocent?" "I cannot tell," said his uncle. "There is no proof. The word of the keeper and the wheelwright stand against the boy's word. If indeed I did believe the one thing or the other, it would be merely a matter of chance, or maybe of sympathy. The boy," he said after a moment, "was my son's playmate, the only other child that I ever knew him to like or to get on with." "Do you," Adam again asked, "hold it possible to her to fulfill your condition?" "Nay, I cannot tell," said the old lord. "To an ordinary person it would not be possible. No ordinary person would ever have taken it on at all. I chose it so. We are not quibbling with the law, Anne-Marie and I."

Adam for a few minutes followed the movement of the small group in the rye. "Will you walk back?" he asked. "No," said his uncle, "I think that I shall stay here till I have seen the end of the thing." "Until sunset?" Adam asked with surprise. "Yes," said the old lord. Adam said: "It will be a long day." "Yes," said his uncle, "a long day. But," he added, as Adam rose to walk away, "if, as you said, you have got that tragedy of which you spoke in your pocket, be as kind as to leave it here, to keep me company." Adam handed him the book.

In the avenue he met two footmen who carried the old lord's morning chocolate down to the pavilion on large silver trays.

As now the sun rose in the sky, and the day grew hot, the lime trees gave forth their exuberance of scent, and the garden was filled with unsurpassed, unbelievable sweetness. Towards the still hour of midday the long avenue reverberated like a soundboard with a low, incessant murmur: the humming of a million bees that clung to the pendulous, thronging clusters of blossoms and were drunk with bliss.

In all the short lifetime of Danish summer there is no richer or more luscious moment than that week wherein the lime trees flower. The heavenly scent goes to the head and to the heart; it seems to unite the fields of Denmark with those of Elysium; it contains both hay, honey and holy incense, and is half fairy-land and half apothecary's locker. The avenue was changed into a mystic edifice, a dryad's cathedral, outward from summit to base lavishly adorned, set with multitudinous ornaments, and golden in the sun. But behind the walls the vaults were benignly cool and sombre, like ambrosial sanctuaries in a dazzling and burning world, and in here the ground was still moist.

Up in the house, behind the silk curtains of the two front windows, the young mistress of the estate from the wide bed stuck her feet into two little high-heeled slippers. Her lace-trimmed nightgown had slid up above her knee and down from the shoulder; her hair, done up in curling-pins for the night, was still frosty with the powder of yesterday, her round face flushed with sleep. She stepped out to the middle of the floor and stood there, looking extremely grave and thoughtful, yet she did not think at all. But through her head a long procession of pictures marched, and she was unconsciously endeavouring to put them in order, as the pictures of her existence had used to be.

She had grown up at Court; it was her world, and there was probably not in the whole country a small creature more exquisitely and innocently drilled to the stately measure of a palace. By favour of the old Dowager Queen she bore her name and that of the King's sister, the Queen of Sweden: Sophie Magdalena. It was with a view to these things that her husband, when he wished to restore his status in high places, had chosen her as a bride, first for his son and then for himself. But her own father, who held an office in the Royal Household and belonged to the new Court aristocracy, in his day had done the same thing the other way round, and had married a country lady, to get a foothold within the old nobility of Denmark. The little girl had her mother's blood in her veins. The country to her had been an immense surprise and delight.

To get into her castle-court she must drive through the farm yard, through the heavy stone gateway in the barn itself, wherein the rolling of her coach for a few seconds re-echoed like thunder. She must drive past the stables and the timber-mare, from which sometimes a miscreant would follow her with sad eyes, and might here startle a long string of squalling geese, or pass the heavy, scowling bull, led on by a ring in his nose and kneading the earth in dumb fury. At first this had been to her, every time, a slight shock and a jest. But after a while all these creatures and things, which belonged to her, seemed to become part of herself. Her mothers, the old Danish country ladies, were robust persons, undismayed by any kind of weather;

now she herself had walked in the rain and had laughed and glowed in it like a green tree.

She had taken her great new home in possession at a time when all the world was unfolding, mating and propagating. Flowers, which she had known only in bouquets and festoons, sprung from the earth round her; birds sang in all the trees. The new-born lambs seemed to her daintier than her dolls had been. From her husband's Hanoverian stud, foals were brought to her to give names; she stood and watched as they poked their soft noses into their mothers' bellies to drink. Of this strange process she had till now only vaguely heard. She had happened to witness, from a path in the park, the rearing and screeching stallion on the mare. All this luxuriance, lust and fecundity was displayed before her eyes, as for her pleasure.

And for her own part, in the midst of it, she was given an old husband who treated her with punctilious respect because she was to bear him a son. Such was the compact; she had known of it from the beginning. Her husband, she found, was doing his best to fulfill his part of it, and she herself was loyal by nature and strictly brought up. She would not shirk her obligation. Only she was vaguely aware of a discord or an incompatibility within her majestic existence, which prevented her from being as happy as she had expected to be.

After a time her chagrin took a strange form: as the consciousness of an absence. Someone ought to have been with her who was not. She had no experience in analysing her feelings; there had not been time for that at Court. Now, as she was more often left to herself, she vaguely probed her own mind. She tried to set her father in that void place, her sisters, her music master, an Italian singer whom she had admired; but none of them would fill it for her. At times she felt lighter at heart, and believed the misfortune to have left her. And then again it would happen, if she were alone, or in her husband's company, and even within his embrace, that everything round her would cry out: Where? Where? so that she let her wild eyes run about the room in search for the being who should have been there, and who had not come.

When, six months ago, she was informed that her first young bridegroom had died and that she was to marry his father in his place, she had not been sorry. Her youthful suitor, the one time she had seen him, had appeared to her infantile and insipid; the father would make a statelier consort. Now she had sometimes thought of the dead boy, and wondered whether with him life would have been more joyful. But she soon again dismissed the picture, and that was the sad youth's last recall to the stage of this world.

Upon one wall of her room there hung a long mirror. As she gazed into it new images came along. The day before, driving with her husband, she had seen, at a distance, a party of village girls bathing in the river, and the sun shining on them. All her life she had moved amongst naked marble deities, but it had till now never occurred to her that the people she knew should themselves be naked under their bodices and trains, waistcoats and satin breeches, that indeed she herself felt naked within her clothes. Now, in front of the looking-glass, she tardily untied the ribbons of her nightgown, and let it drop to the floor.

The room was dim behind the drawn curtains. In the mirror her body was silvery like a white rose; only her cheeks and mouth, and the tips of her fingers and breasts had a faint carmine. Her slender torso was formed by the whalebones that had clasped it tightly from her childhood; above the slim, dimpled knee a gentle narrowness marked the place of her garter. Her limbs were rounded as if, at whatever place they might be cut through with a sharp knife, a perfectly circular transverse incision would be obtained. The side and belly were so smooth that her own gaze slipped and glided, and grasped for a hold. She was not altogether like a statue, she found, and lifted her arms above her head. She turned to get a view of her back, the curves below the waistline were still blushing from the pressure of the bed. She called to mind a few tales about nymphs and goddesses, but they all seemed a long way off, so her mind returned to the peasant girls in the river. They were, for a few minutes, idealized into playmates, or sisters even, since they belonged to her as did the meadow and the blue river itself. And within the next moment the sense of forlornness once more came upon her, a *horror vaccui* like a physical pain. Surely, surely someone should have been with her now, her other self, like the image in the glass, but nearer, stronger, alive. There was no one, the universe was empty round her.

A sudden, keen itching under her knee took her out of her reveries, and awoke in her the hunting instincts of her breed. She wetted a finger on her tongue, slowly brought it down and quickly slapped it to the spot. She felt the diminutive, sharp body of the insect against the silky skin, pressed the thumb to it, and triumphantly lifted up the small prisoner between her fingertips. She stood quite still, as if meditating upon the fact that a flea was the only creature risking its life for her smoothness and sweet blood.

Her maid opened the door and came in, loaded with the attire of the day—shift, stays, hoop and petticoats. She remembered that she had a guest in the house, the new nephew arrived from England. Her husband had instructed her to be kind to their young kinsman, disinherited, so to say, by her presence in the house. They would ride out on the land together.

In the afternoon the sky was no longer blue as in the morning. Large clouds slowly towered up on it, and the great vault itself was colourless, as if diffused into vapours round the white-hot sun in zenith. A low thunder ran along the western horizon; once or twice the dust of the roads rose in tall spirals. But the fields, the hills and the woods were as still as a painted landscape.

Adam walked down the avenue to the pavilion, and found his uncle there, fully dressed, his hands upon his walking-stick and his eyes on the rye field. The book that Adam had given him lay by his side. The field now seemed alive with people. Small groups stood here and there in it, and a long row of men and women were slowly advancing towards the garden in the line of the swath.

The old lord nodded to his nephew, but did not speak or change his position. Adam stood by him as still as himself.

The day to him had been strangely disquieting. At the meeting again with old places the sweet melodies of the past had filled his senses and his mind, and had mingled with new, bewitching tunes of the present. He was back in Denmark, no longer a child but a youth, with a keener sense of the beautiful, with tales of other countries to tell, and still a true son of his own land and enchanted by its loveliness as he had never been before.

But through all these harmonies the tragic and cruel tale which the old lord had told him in the morning, and the sad contest which he knew to be going on so near by, in the corn field, had re-echoed, like the recurrent, hollow throbbing of a muffled drum, a redoubtable sound. It came back time after time, so that he had felt himself to change colour and to answer absently. It brought with it a deeper sense of pity with all that lived than he had ever known. When he had been riding with his young aunt, and their road ran along the scene of the drama, he had taken care to ride between her and the field, so that she should not see what was going on there, or question him about it. He had chosen the way home through the deep, green wood for the same reason.

More dominantly even than the figure of the woman struggling with her sickle for her son's life, the old man's figure, as he had seen it at sunrise, kept him company through the day. He came to ponder on the part which that lonely, determinate form had played in his own life. From the time when his father died, it had impersonated to the boy law and order, wisdom of life and kind guardianship. What was he to do, he thought, if after eighteen years these filial feelings must change, and his second father's figure take on to him a horrible aspect, as a symbol of the tyranny and oppression of the world? What was he to do if ever the two should come to stand in opposition to each other as adversaries?

At the same time an unaccountable, a sinister alarm and dread on behalf of the old man himself took hold of him. For surely here the Goddess Nemesis could not be far away. This man had ruled the world round him for a longer period than Adam's own lifetime and had never been gainsaid by anyone. During the years when he had wandered through Europe with a sick boy of his own blood as his sole companion he had learned to set himself apart from his surroundings, and to close himself up to all outer life, and he had become insusceptible to the ideas and feelings of other human beings. Strange fancies might there have run in his mind, so that in the end he had seen himself as the only person really existing, and the world as a poor and vain shadow-play, which had no substance to it.

Now, in senile wilfullness, he would take in his hand the life of those simpler and weaker than himself, of a woman, using it to his own ends, and he feared of no retributive justice. Did he not know, the young man thought, that there were powers in the world, different from and more formidable than the short-lived might of a despot?

With the sultry heat of the day this foreboding of impending disaster grew upon him, until he felt ruin threatening not the old lord only, but the house, the name and himself with him. It seemed to him that he must cry out a warning to the man he had loved, before it was too late.

But as now he was once more in his uncle's company, the green calm of the garden was so deep that he did not find his voice to cry out. Instead a little French air which his aunt had sung to him up in the house kept running in his mind.—"*C'est un trop doux effort* . . ." He had good knowledge of music; he had heard the air before, in Paris, but not so sweetly sung.

After a time he asked: "Will the woman fulfill her bargain?" His uncle unfolded his hands. "It is an extraordinary thing," he said animatedly, "that it looks as if she might fulfill it. If you count the hours from sunrise till now, and from now till sunset, you will find the time left her to be half of that already gone. And see! She has now mowed two-thirds of the field. But then we will naturally have to reckon with her strength declining as she works on. All in all, it is an idle pursuit in you or me to bet on the issue of the matter; we must wait and see. Sit down, and keep me company in my watch." In two minds Adam sat down.

"And here," said his uncle, and took up the book from the seat, "is your book, which has passed the time finely. It is great poetry, ambrosia to the ear and the heart. And it has, with our discourse on divinity this morning, given me stuff for thought. I have been reflecting upon the law of retributive justice." He took a pinch of snuff, and went on. "A new age," he said, "has made to itself a god in its own image, an emotional god. And now you are already writing a tragedy on your god."

Adam had no wish to begin a debate on poetry with his uncle, but he also somehow dreaded a silence, and said: "It may be, then, that we hold tragedy to be, in the scheme of life, a noble, a divine phenomenon."

"Aye," said his uncle solemnly, "a noble phenomenon, the noblest on earth. But of the earth only, and never divine. Tragedy is the privilege of man, his highest privilege. The God of the Christian Church Himself, when He wished to experience tragedy, had to assume human form. And even at that," he added thoughtfully, "the tragedy was not wholly valid, as it would have become had the hero of it been, in very truth, a man. The divinity of Christ conveyed to it a divine note, the moment of comedy. The real tragic part, by the nature of things, fell to the executors, not to the victim. Nay, my nephew, we should not adulterate the pure elements of the cosmos. Tragedy should remain the right of human beings, subject, in their conditions or in their own nature, to the dire law of necessity. To them it is salvation and beatification. But the gods, whom we must believe to be unacquainted with and incomprehensive of necessity, can have no knowledge of the tragic. When they are brought face to face with it they will, according to my experience, have the good taste and decorum to keep still, and not interfere.

"No," he said after a pause, "the true art of the gods is the comic. The comic is a condescension of the divine to the world of man; it is the sublime vision, which cannot be studied, but must ever be celestially granted. In the comic the gods see their own being reflected as in a mirror, and while the tragic poet is bound by strict laws, they will allow the comic artist a freedom as unlimited as their own. They do not even withhold their own existence from his sports. Jove may favour Lucianos of Samosata. As long as your mockery is in true godly taste you may mock at the gods and still remain a sound devotee. But in pitying, or condoling with your god, you deny and annihilate him, and such is the most horrible of atheisms.

"And here on earth, too," he went on, "we, who stand in lieu of the gods and have emancipated ourselves from the tyranny of necessity, should leave to our vassals their monopoly of tragedy, and for ourselves accept the comic with grace. Only a boorish and cruel master—a parvenu, in fact—will make a jest of his servants' necessity, or force the comic upon them. Only a timid and pedantic ruler, a *petit-maître*, will fear the ludicrous on his own behalf. Indeed," he finished his long speech, "the very same fatality, which, in striking the burgher or peasant, will become tragedy, with the aristocrat is exalted to the comic. By the grace and wit of our acceptance hereof our aristocracy is known."

Adam could not help smiling a little as he heard the apotheosis of the comic on the lips of the erect, ceremonious prophet. In this ironic smile he was, for the first time, estranging himself from the head of his house.

A shadow fell across the landscape. A cloud had crept over the sun; the country changed colour beneath it, faded and bleached, and even all sounds for a minute seemed to die out of it.

"Ah, now," said the old lord, "if it is going to rain, and the rye gets wet, Anne-Marie will not be able to finish in time. And who comes there?" he added, and turned his head a little.

Preceded by a lackey, a man in riding boots and a striped waistcoat with silver buttons, and with his hat in his hand, came down the avenue. He bowed deeply, first to the old lord and then to Adam.

"My bailiff," said the old lord. "Good afternoon, Bailiff. What news have you to bring?" The bailiff made a sad gesture. "Poor news only, my lord," he said. "And how poor news?" asked his master. "There is," said the bailiff with weight, "not a soul at work on the land, and not a sickle going except that of Anne-Marie in this rye field. The mowing has stopped; they are all at her heels. It is a poor day for a first day of the harvest." "Yes, I see," said the old lord. The bailiff went on. "I have spoken kindly to them," he said, "and I have sworn at them; it is all one. They might as well be deaf."

"Good bailiff," said the old lord, "leave them in peace; let them do as they like. This day may, all the same, do them more good than many others. Where is Goske, the boy, Anne-Marie's son?" "We have set him in the small room by the barn," said the bailiff. "Nay, let him be brought down," said the old lord; "let him see his mother at work. But what do you say—will she get the field mowed in time?" "If you ask me, my lord," said the bailiff, "I believe that she will. Who would have thought so? She is only a small woman. It is as hot a day today as, well, as I do ever remember. I myself, you yourself, my lord, could not have done what Anne-Marie has done today." "Nay, nay, we could not, Bailiff," said the old lord.

The bailiff pulled out a red handkerchief and wiped his brow, somewhat calmed by venting his wrath. "If," he remarked with bitterness, "they would all work as the widow works now, we would make a profit on the land." "Yes," said the old lord, and fell into thought, as if calculating the profit it might make. "Still," he said, "as to the question of profit and loss, that is more intricate than it looks. I will tell you something that you may not know: The most famous tissue ever woven was ravelled out again every night. But come," he added, "she is close by now. We will go and have a look at her work ourselves." With these words he rose and set his hat on.

The cloud had drawn away again; the rays of the sun once more burned the wide landcape, and as the small party walked out from under the shade of the trees the dead-still heat was heavy as lead; the sweat sprang out on their faces and their eyelids smarted. On the narrow path they had to go one by one, the old lord stepping along first, all black, and the footman, in his bright livery, bringing up the rear.

The field was indeed filled with people like a market-place;

there were probably a hundred or more men and women in it. To Adam the scene recalled pictures from his Bible: the meeting between Esau and Jacob in Edom, or Boas' reapers in his barley field near Bethlehem. Some were standing by the side of the field, others pressed in small groups close to the mowing woman, and a few followed in her wake, binding up sheaves where she had cut the corn, as if thereby they thought to help her, or as if by all means they meant to have part in her work. A younger woman with a pail on her head kept close to her side, and with her a number of half-grown children. One of these first caught sight of the lord of the estate and his suite, and pointed to him. The binders let their sheaves drop, and as the old man stood still many of the onlookers drew close round him.

The woman on whom till now the eyes of the whole field had rested—a small figure on the large stage—was advancing slowly and unevenly, bent double as if she were walking on her knees, and stumbling as she walked. Her blue head-cloth had slipped back from her head; the grey hair was plastered to the skull with sweat, dusty and stuck with straw. She was obviously totally unaware of the multitude round her; neither did she now once turn her head or her gaze towards the new arrivals.

Absorbed in her work she again and again stretched out her left hand to grasp a handful of corn, and her right hand with the sickle in it to cut it off close to the soil in wavering, groping pulls, like a tired swimmer's strokes. Her course took her so close to the feet of the old lord that his shadow fell on her. Just then she staggered and swayed sideways, and the woman who followed her lifted the pail from her head and held it to her lips. Anne-Marie drank without leaving her hold on her sickle, and the water ran from the corners of her mouth. A boy, close to her, quickly bent one knee, seized her hands in his own and, steadying and guiding them, cut off a gripe of rye. "No, no," said the old lord, "you must not do that, boy. Leave Anne-Marie in peace to her work." At the sound of his voice the woman, falteringly, lifted her face in his direction.

The bony and tanned face was streaked with sweat and dust; the eyes were dimmed. But there was not in its expression the slightest trace of fear or pain. Indeed amongst all the grave and concerned faces of the field hers was the only one perfectly calm, peaceful and mild. The mouth was drawn together in a thin line, a prim, keen, patient little smile, such as will be seen in the face of an old woman at her spinning-wheel or her knitting, eager on her work, and happy in it. And as the younger woman lifted back the pail, she immediately again fell to her mowing, with an ardent, tender craving, like that of a mother who lays a baby to the nipple. Like an insect that bustles along in high grass, or like a small vessel in a heavy sea, she butted her way on, her quiet face once more bent upon her task.

The whole throng of onlookers, and with them the small group from the pavilion, advanced as she advanced, slowly and as if drawn by a string. The bailiff, who felt the intense silence of the field heavy on him, said to the old lord: "The rye will yield better this year than last," and got no reply. He repeated his remark to Adam, and at last to the footman, who felt himself above a discussion on agriculture, and only cleared his throat in answer. In a while the bailiff again broke the silence. "There is the boy," he said and pointed with his thumb. "They have brought him down." At that moment the woman fell forward on her face and was lifted up by those nearest to her.

Adam suddenly stopped on the path, and covered his eyes with his hand. The old lord without turning asked him if he felt incommoded by the heat. "No," said Adam, "but stay. Let me speak to you." His uncle stopped, with his hand on the stick and looking ahead, as if regretful of being held back.

"In the name of God," cried the young man in French, "force not this woman to continue." There was a short pause. "But I force her not, my friend," said his uncle in the same language. "She is free to finish at any moment." "At the cost of her child only," again cried Adam. "Do you not see that she is dying? You know not what you are doing, or what it may bring upon you."

The old lord, perplexed by this unexpected animadversion, after a second turned all round, and his pale, clear eyes sought his nephew's face with stately surprise. His long, waxen face, with two symmetrical curls at the sides, had something of the mien of an idealized and ennobled old sheep or ram. He made sign to the bailiff to go on. The footman also withdrew a little, and the uncle and nephew were, so to say, alone on the path. For a minute neither of them spoke.

"In this very place where we now stand," said the old lord, then, with hauteur, "I gave Anne-Marie my word."

"My uncle!" said Adam. "A life is a greater thing even than a word. Recall that word, I beseech you, which was given in caprice, as a whim. I am praying you more for your sake than for my own, yet I shall be grateful to you all my life if you will grant me my prayer."

"You will have learned in school," said his uncle, "that in the beginning was the word. It may have been pronounced in caprice, as a whim, the Scripture tells us nothing about it. It is still the principle of our world, its law of gravitation. My own humble word has been the principle of the land on which we stand, for an age of man. My father's word was the same, before my day."

"You are mistaken," cried Adam. "The word is creative—it is imagination, daring and passion. By it the world was made. How much greater are these powers which bring into being than any restricting or controlling law! You wish the land on which we look to produce and propagate; you should not banish from it the forces which cause, and which keep up life, nor turn it into a desert by dominance of law. And when you look at the people, simpler than we and nearer to the heart of nature, who do not analyse their feelings, whose life is one with the life of the earth, do they not inspire in you tenderness, respect, reverence even? This woman is ready to die for her son; will it ever happen to you or me that a woman willingly gives up her life for us? And if it did indeed come to pass, should we make so light of it as not to give up a dogma in return?"

"You are young," said the old lord. "A new age will undoubtedly applaud you. I am old-fashioned, I have been quoting to you texts a thousand years old. We do not, perhaps, quite understand one another. But with my own people I am, I believe, in good understanding. Anne-Marie might well feel that I am making light of her exploit, if now, at the eleventh hour, I did nullify it by a second word. I myself should feel so in her place. Yes, my nephew, it is possible, did I grant you your prayer and pronounce such an amnesty, that I should find it void against her faithfulness, and that we would still see her at her work, unable to give it up, as a shuttle in the rye field, until she had it all mowed. But she would then be a shocking, a horrible sight, a figure of unseemly fun, like a small planet running wild in the sky, when the law of gravitation had been done away with."

"And if she dies at her task," Adam exclaimed, "her death and its consequences will come upon your head."

The old lord took off his hat and gently ran his hand over his powdered head. "Upon my head?" he said. "I have kept up my head in many weathers. Even," he added proudly, "against the cold wind from high places. In what shape will it come upon my head, my nephew?" "I cannot tell," cried Adam in despair. "I have spoken to warn you. God only knows." "Amen," said the old lord with a little delicate smile. "Come, we will walk on." Adam drew in his breath deeply.

"No," he said in Danish. "I cannot come with you. This field is yours; things will happen here as you decide. But I myself must go away. I beg you to let me have, this evening, a coach as far as town. For I could not sleep another night under your roof, which I have honoured beyond any on earth." So many conflicting feelings at his own speech thronged in his breast that it would have been impossible for him to give them words.

The old lord, who had already begun to walk on, stood still, and with him the lackey. He did not speak for a minute, as if to give Adam time to collect his mind. But the young man's mind was in uproar and would not be collected.

"Must we," the old man asked, in Danish, "take leave here, in the rye field? I have held you dear, next to my own son. I have followed your career in life from year to year, and have been proud of you. I was happy when you wrote to say that you were coming back. If now you will go away, I wish you well." He shifted his walking-stick from the right hand to the left and gravely looked his nephew in the face.

Adam did not meet his eyes. He was gazing out over the landscape. In the late mellow afternoon it was resuming its colours, like a painting brought into proper light; in the meadows the little black stacks of peat stood gravely distinct upon the green sward. On this same morning he had greeted it all, like a child running laughingly to its mother's bosom; now already he must tear himself from it, in discordance, and forever. And at the moment of parting it seemed infinitely dearer than any time before, so much beautified and solemnized by the coming separation that it looked like the place in a dream, a landscape out of paradise, and he wondered if it was really the same. But, yes—there before him was, once more, the hunting-ground of long ago. And there was the road on which he had ridden today.

"But tell me where you mean to go from here," said the old lord slowly. "I myself have travelled a good deal in my days. I know the word of leaving, the wish to go away. But I have learned by experience that, in reality, the word has a meaning only to the place and the people which one leaves. When you have left my house—although it will see you go with sadness—as far as it is concerned the matter is finished and done with. But to the person who goes away it is a different thing, and not so simple. At the moment that he leaves one place he will be already, by the laws of life, on his way to another, upon this earth. Let me know, then, for the sake of our old acquaintance, to which place you are going when you leave here. To England?"

"No," said Adam. He felt in his heart that he could never again go back to England or to his easy and carefree life there. It was not far enough away; deeper waters than the North Sea must now be laid between him and Denmark. "No, not to England," he said. "I shall go to America, to the new world." For a moment he shut his eyes, trying to form to himself a picture of existence in America, with the grey Atlantic Ocean between him and these fields and woods.

"To America?" said his uncle and drew up his eyebrows. "Yes, I have heard of America. They have got freedom there, a big waterfall, savage red men. They shoot turkeys, I have read, as we shoot partridges. Well, if it be your wish, go to America, Adam, and be happy in the new world."

He stood for some time, sunk in thought, as if he had already sent off the young man to America, and had done with him. When at last he spoke, his words had the character of a monologue, enunciated by the person who watches things come and go, and himself stays on.

"Take service, there," he said, "with the power which will give you an easier bargain than this: That with your own life you may buy the life of your son."

Adam had not listened to his uncle's remarks about America, but the conclusive, solemn words caught his ear. He looked up. As if for the first time in his life, he saw the old man's figure as a whole, and conceived how small it was, so much smaller than himself, pale, a thin black anchorite upon his own land. A thought ran through his head: "How terrible to be old!" The abhorrence of the tyrant, and the sinister dread on his behalf, which had followed him all day, seemed to die out of him, and his pity with all creation to extend even to the sombre form before him.

His whole being had cried out for harmony. Now, with the possibility of forgiving, of a reconciliation, a sense of relief went through him; confusedly he bethought himself of Anne-Marie drinking the water held to her lips. He took off his hat, as his uncle had done a moment ago, so that to a beholder at a distance it would seem that the two dark-clad gentlemen on the path were repeatedly and respectfully saluting one another, and brushed the hair from his forehead. Once more the tune of the garden-room rang in his mind:

Mourir pour ce qu'on aime
C'est un trop doux effort . . .

He stood for a long time immobile and dumb. He broke off a few ears of rye, kept them in his hand and looked at them.

He saw the ways of life, he thought, as a twined and tangled design, complicated and mazy; it was not given him or any mortal to command or control it. Life and death, happiness and woe, the past and the present, were interlaced within the pattern. Yet to the initiated it might be read as easily as our ciphers—which to the savage must seem confused and incomprehensible—will be read by the schoolboy. And out of the contrasting elements concord rose. All that lived must suffer; the old man, whom he had judged hardly, had suffered, as he had watched his son die, and had dreaded the obliteration of his being. He himself would come to know ache, tears and remorse, and, even through these, the fullness of life. So might now, to the woman in the rye field, her ordeal be a triumphant procession. For to die for the one you loved was an effort too sweet for words.

As now he thought of it, he knew that all his life he had sought the unity of things, the secret which connects the phenomena of existence. It was this strife, this dim presage, which had sometimes made him stand still and inert in the midst of the games of his playfellows, or which had, at other moments—on moonlight nights, or in his little boat on the sea—lifted the boy to ecstatic happiness. Where other young people, in their pleasures or their amours, had searched for contrast and variety, he himself had yearned only to comprehend in full the oneness of the world. If things had come differently to him, if his young cousin had not died, and the events that followed his death had not brought him to Denmark, his search for understanding and harmony might have taken him to America, and he might have found them there, in the virgin forests of a new world. Now they have been disclosed to him today, in the place where he had played as a child. As the song is one with the voice that sings it, as the road is one with the goal, as lovers are made one in their embrace, so is man one with his destiny, and he shall love it as himself.

He looked up again, towards the horizon. If he wished to, he felt, he might find out what it was that had brought to him, here, the sudden conception of the unity of the universe. When this same morning he had philosophized, lightly and for his own sake, on his feeling of belonging to this land and soil, it had been the beginning of it. But since then it had grown; it had become a mightier thing, a revelation to his soul. Some time he would look into it, for the law of cause and effect was a wonderful and fascinating study. But not now. This hour was consecrated to greater emotions, to a surrender to fate and to the will of life.

"No," he said at last. "If you wish it I shall not go. I shall stay here."

At that moment a long, loud roll of thunder broke the stillness of the afternoon. It re-echoed for a while amongst the low hills, and it reverberated within the young man's breast as powerfully as if he had been seized and shaken by hands. The landscape had spoken. He remembered that twelve hours ago he had put a question to it, half in jest, and not knowing what he did. Here it gave him its answer.

What it contained he did not know; neither did he inquire. In his promise to his uncle he had given himself over to the mightier powers of the world. Now what must come must come.

"I thank you," said the old lord, and made a little stiff gesture with his hand. "I am happy to hear you say so. We should not let the difference in our ages, or of our views, separate us. In our family we have been wont to keep peace and faith with one another. You have made my heart lighter."

Something within his uncle's speech faintly recalled to Adam the misgivings of the afternoon. He rejected them; he would not let them trouble the new, sweet felicity which his resolution to stay had brought him.

"I shall go on now," said the old lord. "But there is no need for you to follow me. I will tell you tomorrow how the matter has ended." "No," said Adam, "I shall come back by sunset, to see the end of it myself."

All the same he did not come back. He kept the hour in his

mind, and all through the evening the consciousness of the drama, and the profound concern and compassion with which, in his thoughts, he followed it, gave to his speech, glance and movements a grave and pathetic substance. But he felt that he was, in the rooms of the manor, and even by the harpsichord on which he accompanied his aunt to her air from *Alceste*, as much in the centre of things as if he had stood in the rye field itself, and as near to those human beings whose fate was now decided there. Anne-Marie and he were both in the hands of destiny, and destiny would, by different ways, bring each to the designated end.

Later on he remembered what he had thought that evening.

But the old lord stayed on. Late in the afternoon he even had an idea; he called down his valet to the pavilion and made him shift his clothes on him and dress him up in a brocaded suit that he had worn at Court. He let a lace-trimmed shirt be drawn over his head and stuck out his slim legs to have them put into thin silk stockings and buckled shoes. In this majestic attire he dined alone, of a frugal meal, but took a bottle of Rhenish wine with it, to keep up his strength. He sat on for a while, a little sunk in his seat; then, as the sun neared the earth, he straightened himself, and took the way down to the field.

The shadows were now lengthening, azure blue along all the eastern slopes. The lonely trees in the corn marked their site by narrow blue pools running out from their feet, and as the old man walked a thin, immensely elongated reflection stirred behind him on the path. Once he stood still; he thought he heard a lark singing over his head, a spring-like sound; his tired head held no clear perception of the season; he seemed to be walking, and standing, in a kind of eternity.

The people in the field were no longer silent, as they had been in the afternoon. Many of them talked loudly among themselves, and a little farther away a woman was weeping.

When the bailiff saw his master, he came up to him. He told him, in great agitation, that the widow would, in all likelihood, finish the mowing of the field within a quarter of an hour.

"Are the keeper and the wheelwright here?" the old lord asked him. "They have been here," said the bailiff, "and have gone away, five times. Each time they have said that they would not come back. But they have come back again, all the same, and they are here now." "And where is the boy?" the old lord asked again. "He is with her," said the bailiff. "I have given him leave to follow her. He has walked close to his mother all the afternoon, and you will see him now by her side, down there."

Anne-Marie was now working her way up towards them more evenly than before, but with extreme slowness, as if at any moment she might come to a stand-still. This excessive tardiness, the old lord reflected, if it had been purposely performed, would have been an inimitable, dignified exhibition of skilled art; one might fancy the Emperor of China advancing in like manner on a divine procession or rite. He shaded his eyes with his hand, for the sun was now just beyond the horizon, and its last rays made light, wild, many-coloured specks dance before his sight. With such splendour did the sunset emblazon the earth and the air that the landscape was turned into a melting-pot of glorious metals. The meadows and the grasslands became pure gold; the barley field near by, with its long ears, was a live lake of shining silver.

There was only a small patch of straw standing in the rye field, when the woman, alarmed by the change in the light, turned her head a little to get a look at the sun. The while she did not stop her work, but grasped one handful of corn and cut it off, then another, and another. A great stir, and a sound like a manifold, deep sigh, ran through the crowd. The field was now mowed from one end to the other. Only the mower herself did not realize the fact; she stretched out her hand anew, and when she found nothing in it, she seemed puzzled or disappointed. Then she let her arms drop, and slowly sank to her knees.

Many of the women burst out weeping, and the swarm drew close round her, leaving only a small open space at the side where the old lord stood. Their sudden nearness frightened Anne-Marie; she made a slight, uneasy movement, as if terrified that they should put their hands on her.

The boy, who had kept by her all day, now fell on his knees beside her. Even he dared not touch her, but held one arm low behind her back and the other before her, level with her collarbone, to catch hold of her if she should fall, and all the time he cried aloud. At that moment the sun went down.

The old lord stepped forward and solemnly took off his hat. The crowd became silent, waiting for him to speak. But for a minute or two he said nothing. Then he addressed her, very slowly.

"Your son is free, Anne-Marie," he said. He again waited a little, and added: "You have done a good day's work, which will long be remembered."

Anne-Marie raised her gaze only as high as his knees, and he understood that she had not heard what he said. He turned to the boy. "You tell your mother, Goske," he said, gently, "what I have told her."

The boy had been sobbing wildly, in raucous, broken moans. It took him some time to collect and control himself. But when at last he spoke, straight into his mother's face, his voice was low, a little impatient, as if he were conveying an everyday message to her. "I am free, Mother," he said. "You have done a good day's work that will long be remembered."

At the sound of his voice she lifted her face to him. A faint, bland shadow of surprise ran over it, but still she gave no sign of having heard what he said, so that the people round them began to wonder if the exhaustion had turned her deaf. But after a moment she slowly and waveringly raised her hand, fumbling in the air as she aimed at his face, and with her fingers touched his cheek. The cheek was wet with tears, so that at the contact her fingertips lightly stuck to it, and she seemed unable to overcome the infinitely slight resistance, or to withdraw her hand. For a minute the two looked each other in the face. Then, softly and lingeringly, like a sheaf of corn that falls to the ground, she sank forward onto the boy's shoulder, and he closed his arms round her.

He held her thus, pressed against him, his own face buried in her hair and head-cloth, for such a long time that those nearest to them, frightened because her body looked so small in his embrace, drew closer, bent down and loosened his grip. The boy let them do so without a word or a movement. But the woman who held Anne-Marie, in her arms to lift her up, turned her face to the old lord. "She is dead," she said.

The people who had followed Anne-Marie all through the day kept standing and stirring in the field for many hours, as long as the evening light lasted, and longer. Long after some of them had made a stretcher from branches of the trees and had carried away the dead woman, others wandered on, up and down the stubble, imitating and measuring her course from one end of the rye field to the other, and binding up the last sheaves, where she had finished her mowing.

The old lord stayed with them for a long time, stepping along a little, and again standing still.

In the place where the woman had died the old lord later on had a stone set up, with a sickle engraved in it. The peasants on the land then named the rye field "Sorrow-Acre." By this name it was known a long time after the story of the woman and her son had itself been forgotten.

Interpretive Questions

1. Why does the old lord give Anne-Marie a chance to save her son?
2. Why does Adam change his mind about going to America?
3. Is Adam correct in thinking his uncle is using Anne-Marie for his own ends?
4. Why does the old lord think that tragedy is the highest privilege of human beings?
5. Why does Anne-Marie seem calm, happy, and eager in her task? Why does she seem disappointed when she is through?

Questions of Fact, Interpretation, and Evaluation

Three kinds of questions are asked about a selection in shared inquiry: questions of fact, questions of interpretation, and questions of evaluation.

Questions of fact ask you to recall something in the selection, using your own words or the words of the author. A question of fact has only one correct answer.

Questions of interpretation ask you to offer your opinion about what the selection means. Unlike a question of fact, a question of interpretation usually has more than one correct answer.

Questions of evaluation ask you whether you agree or disagree with what the author said or whether something in the selection has application to your own life. You support your answer to a question of evaluation by talking about your own values or your own experiences rather than about the selection itself.

Since interpreting literature is the main purpose of the Great Books program, discussion focuses on questions of interpretation. Factual questions are used to bring out evidence in support of interpretations. Questions of evaluation are asked only after the meaning of a selection has been clarified through discussion.

This exercise will give you practice in distinguishing questions of fact, interpretation, and evaluation. In the blank before each of the following questions, write (F) if the question is FACTUAL, (I) if it is INTERPRETIVE, or (E) if it is EVALUATIVE. If you are in doubt about how to classify any question, refer to the selection.

____ 1. Why is Adam given a slight limp?

____ 2. Why did the old lord marry again?

____ 3. What does the old lord mean when he says, "We are not quibbling with the law, Anne-Marie and I"?

____ 4. Does the old lord believe Goske is guilty or innocent of the crime of which he is accused?

____ 5. Why does the old lord set Anne-Marie a task that is almost impossible?

____ 6. Is tragedy the highest privilege of human beings?

____ 7. Why does Adam lack ambition to head the family?

____ 8. Can human beings emancipate themselves from the "tyranny of necessity"?

____ 9. Why does Adam return to Denmark?

____ 10. Was Adam wrong in asking his uncle whether he should stay or leave?

IX

By and About Alexis de Tocqueville

(1805–1859)

From May 1831 to February 1832, Alexis de Tocqueville observed democratic politics and society as he traveled in the United States. *Democracy in America,* the record of his observations, brought Tocqueville international recognition.

After a month of travel, Tocqueville wrote to his father about the relative value of political institutions:

> The more I see this country the more I admit myself penetrated with this truth: that there is nothing absolute in the theoretical value of political institutions, and that their efficiency depends almost always on the original circumstances and the social condition of the people to whom they are applied. I see institutions succeed here which would infallibly turn France upside down; others which suit us would obviously do harm in America; and yet, either I am much mistaken, or man is neither other nor better here than with us. Only he is otherwise placed.

In *Democracy in America,* he commented on self-interest in relation to morality:

> The principle of self-interest rightly understood produces no great acts of self-sacrifice, but it suggests daily small acts of self-denial. By itself it cannot suffice to make a man virtuous; but it disciplines a number of persons in habits of regularity, temperance, moderation, foresight, self-command; and if it does not lead men straight to virtue by the will, it gradually draws them in that direction by their habits. . . . The principle of interest rightly understood perhaps prevents men from rising far above the level of mankind, but a great number of other men, who were falling far below it, are caught and restrained by it. Observe some few individuals, they are lowered by it; survey mankind, they are raised.

On majority rule:

> A majority taken collectively is only an individual whose opinions, and frequently whose interests, are opposed to those of another individual who is styled a minority. If it be admitted that a man

> possessing absolute power may misuse that power by wronging his adversaries, why should not a majority be liable to the same reproach?

On reelecting the president:

> It is impossible to consider the ordinary course of affairs in the United States without perceiving that the desire to be re-elected is the chief aim of the President; that the whole policy of his administration, and even his most indifferent measures, tend to this object; and that, especially as the crisis approaches, his personal interest takes the place of his interest in the public good. The principle of re-eligibility renders the corrupting influence of elective government still more extensive and pernicious.

In the selection from *Democracy in America* that follows, Tocqueville notes that Americans, although the most prosperous people on earth, are too restless to enjoy the abundance which surrounds them. Insatiable ambition and the freedom to pursue it contribute to this situation. But the real problem is equality: when the major distinctions among people are eliminated, the minor differences become more noticeable—and less tolerable. In this way, equality itself breeds an insatiable longing for even greater equality.

Why Americans Are Often So Restless

Alexis de Tocqueville

In certain remote corners of the Old World you may sometimes stumble upon little places which seem to have been forgotten among the general tumult and which have stayed still while all around them moves. The inhabitants are mostly very ignorant and very poor; they take no part in affairs of government, and often governments oppress them. But yet they seem serene and often have a jovial disposition.

In America I have seen the freest and best educated of men in circumstances the happiest to be found in the world; yet it seemed to me that a cloud habitually hung on their brow, and they seemed serious and almost sad even in their pleasures.

The chief reason for this is that the former do not give a moment's thought to the ills they endure, whereas the latter never stop thinking of the good things they have not got.

It is odd to watch with what feverish ardor the Americans pursue prosperity and how they are ever tormented by the

---

*A selection from *Democracy in America*.

shadowy suspicion that they may not have chosen the shortest route to get it.

Americans cleave to the things of this world as if assured that they will never die, and yet are in such a rush to snatch any that come within their reach, as if expecting to stop living before they have relished them. They clutch everything but hold nothing fast, and so lose grip as they hurry after some new delight.

An American will build a house in which to pass his old age and sell it before the roof is on; he will plant a garden and rent it just as the trees are coming into bearing; he will clear a field and leave others to reap the harvest; he will take up a profession and leave it, settle in one place and soon go off elsewhere with his changing desires. If his private business allows him a moment's relaxation, he will plunge at once into the whirlpool of politics. Then, if at the end of a year crammed with work he has a little spare leisure, his restless curiosity goes with him traveling up and down the vast territories of the United States. Thus he will travel five hundred miles in a few days as a distraction from his happiness.

Death steps in in the end and stops him before he has grown tired of this futile pursuit of that complete felicity which always escapes him.

At first sight there is something astonishing in this spectacle of so many lucky men restless in the midst of abundance. But it is a spectacle as old as the world; all that is new is to see a whole people performing in it.

The taste for physical pleasures must be regarded as the first cause of this secret restlessness betrayed by the actions of the Americans, and of the inconstancy of which they give daily examples.

A man who has set his heart on nothing but the good things of this world is always in a hurry, for he has only a limited time in which to find them, get them, and enjoy them. Remembrance of the shortness of life continually goads him on. Apart from the goods he has, he thinks of a thousand others which death will prevent him from tasting if he does not hurry. This thought fills him with distress, fear, and regret and keeps his mind continually in agitation, so that he is always changing his plans and his abode.

Add to this taste for prosperity a social state in which neither law nor custom holds anyone in one place, and that is a great further stimulus to this restlessness of temper. One will then find people continually changing path for fear of missing the shortest cut leading to happiness.

It is, moreover, easy to understand that although those whose passions are bent on physical pleasures are eager in their desires, they are also easily discouraged. For as their ultimate object is enjoyment, the means to it must be prompt and easy, for otherwise the trouble of getting the pleasure would be greater than the pleasure when won. Hence the prevailing temper is at the same time ardent and soft, violent and enervated. Men are often less afraid of death than of enduring effort toward one goal.

Equality leads by a still shorter path to the various effects I have just described.

When all prerogatives of birth and fortune are abolished, when all professions are open to all and a man's own energies may bring him to the top of any of them, an ambitious man may think it easy to launch on a great career and feel that he is called to no common destiny. But that is a delusion which experience quickly corrects. The same equality which allows each man to entertain vast hopes makes each man by himself weak. His power is limited on every side, though his longings may wander where they will.

Not only are men powerless by themselves, but at every step

they find immense obstacles which they had not at first noticed.

They have abolished the troublesome privileges of some of their fellows, but they come up against the competition of all. The barrier has changed shape rather than place. When men are more or less equal and are following the same path, it is very difficult for any of them to walk faster and get out beyond the uniform crowd surrounding and hemming them in.

This constant strife between the desires inspired by equality and the means it supplies to satisfy them harasses and wearies the mind.

One can imagine men who have found a degree of liberty completely satisfactory to them. In that case they will enjoy their independence without anxiety or excitement. But men will never establish an equality which will content them.

No matter how a people strives for it, all the conditions of life can never be perfectly equal. Even if, by misfortune, such an absolute dead level were attained, there would still be inequalities of intelligence which, coming directly from God, will ever escape the laws of man.

No matter, therefore, how democratic the social condition and political constitution of a people may be, one can be sure that each and every citizen will be aware of dominating positions near him, and it is a safe guess that he will always be looking doggedly just in that direction. When inequality is the general rule in society, the greatest inequalities attract no attention. When everything is more or less level, the slightest variation is noticed. Hence the more equal men are, the more insatiable will be their longing for equality.

Among democratic peoples men easily obtain a certain equality, but they will never get the sort of equality they long for. That is a quality which ever retreats before them without getting quite out of sight, and as it retreats it beckons them on to pursue. Every instant they think they will catch it, and each time it slips through their fingers. They see it close enough to know its charms, but they do not get near enough to enjoy it, and they will be dead before they have fully relished its delights.

That is the reason for the strange melancholy often haunting inhabitants of democracies in the midst of abundance, and of that disgust with life sometimes gripping them in calm and easy circumstances.

In France we are worried about the increasing rate of suicides; in America suicide is rare, but I am told that madness is commoner than anywhere else.

Those are different symptoms of the same malady.

The Americans do not kill themselves, however distressed they may be, because their religion forbids them to do so and because materialist philosophy is practically unknown to them, although the passion for prosperity is general.

Their will resists, but reason frequently gives way.

In democratic times enjoyments are more lively than in times of aristocracy, and more especially, immeasurably greater numbers taste them. But, on the other hand, one must admit that hopes and desires are much more often disappointed, minds are more anxious and on edge, and trouble is felt more keenly.

Interpretive Questions

1. Does Tocqueville think Americans are unhappy because they have a mistaken view of happiness?
2. Why does a society devoted to equal opportunity weaken each individual?
3. Why does Tocqueville think absolutely equal conditions of life would be a misfortune?
4. According to Tocqueville, how should people live to be happy?
5. Does Tocqueville think Americans are restless because they don't know what they want or because what they want is not attainable?

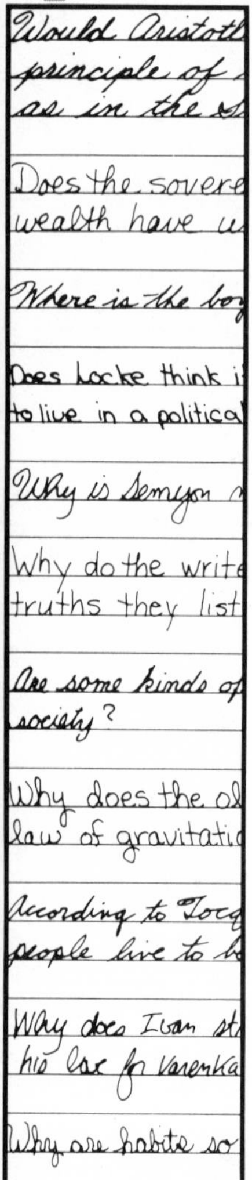

Developing Interpretive Questions

The more you participate in Great Books discussions, the more you will see problems of meaning in the selections you read. Some of your notes may already be in the form of interpretive questions; others can be developed into questions.

Writing interpretive questions from your notes will help you to prepare for discussion. Remember that an interpretive question is a question you care about that can be explored using the text everyone has read. It has more than one possible correct answer.

The most likely sources of interpretive questions are listed here, together with the questions one reader developed from her responses to Tocqueville's essay.

What seems important. Very early in the selection Tocqueville comments that Americans seem serious and almost sad in spite of their advantages, then goes on to say that this is because they "never stop thinking of the good things they have not got." The reader wondered whether Tocqueville thought Americans simply didn't have the right idea about what happiness is, so she asked this question:

> Does Tocqueville think that Americans are unhappy because they have a mistaken view of happiness?

What you don't understand. The reader did not understand Tocqueville's observation that Americans take long vacations as distractions from happiness, so she asked this question:

> Why does Tocqueville call traveling five hundred miles on a few days' vacation "a distraction from happiness"?

What you agree or disagree with. The reader disagreed with Tocqueville's statement that it would be a misfortune if all the conditions of life were perfectly equal for everyone. It seemed to her that it would be ideal if differences were erased and everyone had an equal chance for a happy and productive life. She wrote this question because of her disagreement with Tocqueville:

> Why does Tocqueville think that perfect equality of the conditions of life would be a misfortune?

What the author seems to emphasize. Tocqueville continually stresses the Americans' restlessness and unhappiness in spite of their fondness for material things. The author's emphasis led the reader to this question:

> Does Tocqueville think a "taste for property" is incompatible with happiness?

X

By and About Leo Tolstoy

(1828–1910)

Early in his career, when he was writing *War and Peace,* Tolstoy felt that the purpose of art was incompatible with social reform:

> If I were to be told that I could write a novel whereby I might irrefutably establish what seems to me the correct point of view on all social problems, I would not even devote two hours' work to such a novel, but if I were to be told that what I should write would be read in twenty years' time by those who are now children, and that they would laugh and cry over it and love life, I would devote all my energies to it.

Later in life he experienced a religious crisis that resulted in a sharp change in goals and values. At first he returned to the Russian Orthodox Church; later he proclaimed a heretical Christianity that denied the divinity of Christ and stressed humility, chastity, the abandonment of private property, nonviolent resistance to evil, and universal brotherhood. He signed over his property to his wife, dressed as a peasant and labored in the fields, became a vegetarian, and generally tried to live without exploiting the labor of others. Although he did not completely abandon literature, he spent most of his energy writing tracts instructing his contemporaries how to live. In a self-portrait for the amusement of his family, he wrote:

> Leo Nikolayevich Tolstoy. Sanguine temperament. His delusion is that he can change others' lives with words. General symptoms: dissatisfaction with the present scheme of things; blames everyone except himself; voluble irritability, no consideration for his listeners; often goes through phases of manic excitement, giving way to exaggerated and lachrymose sentimentality. . . . Particular symptoms: indulges in irrelevant activities: polishes and repairs shoes, mows hay and so forth.

Maxim Gorky described Tolstoy's gift for seeing experience from several angles at once. On a walk with a friend, Tolstoy noticed two soldiers approaching in the distance, the metal of their uniforms gleaming in the sun, their spurs jingling, keeping step like one man, their faces shining with the self-assurance of youth:

> Tolstoy began to grumble at them: "What pompous stupidity! Like animals trained to the whip. . . ." But when the guardsmen came abreast with him, he stopped, followed them caressingly with his eyes and said enthusiastically: "How handsome! Old Romans, eh, Liovushka? Their strength and beauty? Oh Lord! How charming it is when men are handsome, how charming!"

After the Ball

Leo Tolstoy

So you would say that by himself a man cannot tell good from evil, that it's all a question of environment, that we are prey to our environment. But for my part I think it's all a matter of chance. Take my own case . . ."

This was how our highly respected friend, Ivan Vasilevich, began talking. We had been having a conversation to the effect that if ever the individual man were to be improved, one would have first of all to change the conditions in which people live. Now no one had actually said that it wasn't possible for a man by himself to tell good from evil, but Ivan Vasilevich had a way of responding to his own ideas as they were prompted by conversations and of using them as a pretext to relate episodes from his own life. Often, because he used to tell his story with such frankness and honesty, he would become quite engrossed in it and forget completely what had moved him to begin. This is what happened this time too.

"I'll tell you about my own case. My whole life was shaped the way it is, rather than any other, not by environment, but by something quite different."

"By what then?" we asked.

"Well, it's a long story. I'll need some time to make you understand."

"Go ahead, we're listening."

Ivan Vasilevich thought for a moment, then shook his head.

"Yes," he said. "From that one night, or rather that one morning onwards my whole life changed."

"So what happened then?"

"It happened that I was very much in love. I had fallen in love many times, but this was my greatest love. It's all over now; her daughters are already married. It was Varenka, yes, Varenka B." (Ivan Vasilevich gave her surname.) "Even at the age of fifty she was a remarkably beautiful woman. But in her youth, at eighteen, she was captivating: tall, slim, graceful, and regal, quite regal. She always carried herself extraordinarily erect, as if this were the only way possible for her, and her beauty and height, along with her habit of tilting her head back slightly, gave her an air of majesty, in spite of her thinness, or rather skinniness. This would have frightened people away from her, had it not been for the tender, invariably merry smile on her lips and in her brilliant, captivating eyes, and in the whole of her lovely young being."

"Just listen to how he describes her!"

"Yes, and however I describe her, I'll never be able to make you understand what she was like. But that doesn't matter. What I want to tell you about happened in the forties. At that time I was a student at a provincial university. I don't know whether it was a good thing or bad thing, but in our university at that time there were no philosophical circles and no theories, we were simply young, and we lived as young people do:

we worked and we had a good time. I was a high-spirited and very lively young fellow, and rich into the bargain. I owned a fine thoroughbred, and I used to go tobogganing down the hills with the girls—skates were not yet in fashion; and I lived it up with my friends—we drank nothing but champagne at that time; if we didn't have any money, we drank nothing, but we didn't drink vodka like they do now. I enjoyed most of all going to *soirées* and balls. I could dance very well and was quite good-looking."

"Come now, there's no need to be modest," interrupted one of the women present. "We all know your picture, don't we? You were not just quite good-looking, you were very handsome."

"Handsome or not, that's not important. What is important, though, is that during the time my love for her was at its height, just before the beginning of Lent, I was at a ball given by the marshal of our province. He was a kindly old man, a generous host, and he held a position at court. His wife was equally kindly and, standing to receive her guests in a low-cut, brown velvet dress which left her plump, elderly white shoulders bare and wearing a diamond frontlet in her hair, she looked like portraits one sees of the Empress Elizabeth. The ball was wonderful. There was a splendid room where the musicians—the then highly acclaimed serf-orchestra of a local landowner-patron—had a gallery to themselves and where there was a magnificent buffet and an overflowing sea of champagne. Although I was a devotee of champagne, I didn't drink, because even without wine I was drunk with love, but to make up for it I danced until I was dropping—quadrilles, waltzes, and polkas—and of course as many of them as possible with Varenka. She was wearing a white dress with a pink sash, white kid gloves reaching almost to her thin pointed elbows, and white satin shoes. I was robbed of the mazurka: a quite repulsive engineer, Anisimov—I haven't yet been able to forgive him for what he did—had asked her for the dance as soon as she came into the room, whilst I had called in at my barber's for a pair of gloves and was late. So I didn't dance the mazurka with her, but with a German girl in whom I had taken some interest previously. But I fear on that evening I was very impolite to her, I didn't talk to her and didn't look at her; I had eyes only for that tall, slim figure in the white dress with its pink sash, for Varenka's radiant, flushed face and her lovely tender eyes. Not only I, but everyone else was looking at her and admiring her, men and women alike, even though she put them all in the shade. It was impossible not to admire her.

"According to the rules, so to speak, I shouldn't have danced the mazurka with her, but in fact I danced with her almost the whole time. She would come boldly forward across the whole length of the room straight to me, and I would jump up without waiting for an invitation, and she would thank me with a smile for my quick-wittedness. Whenever our row was led up to hers, and she miscalculated my position in the set, she would give her hand to one of the other men, shrugging her thin little shoulders, and smile at me as a token of regret and consolation. Whenever there was a waltz figure in the mazurka, I waltzed with her for a long time. Breathing fast, she would smile and say *'Encore.'* And I waltzed with her over and over again and could not feel my body."

"What do you mean, you couldn't feel it? When you put your arms around her waist I think you must have felt a lot, not only your own body, but hers too," said one of the guests.

Ivan Vasilevich suddenly blushed, and almost shouted in anger:

"Yes, that's just like you young people nowadays. You see nothing apart from a woman's body. It was not like that in our day. The more passionately I was in love, the less physical she became for me. Today you see legs, and ankles, and things like that, you undress the woman you love, for me, though, as Alphonse Karr said—and what a fine writer he was—the object of my love was always clad in bronze. Far from undressing those we love, we strove, like the good son of Noah, to cover up their nakedness. But you wouldn't understand any of that."

"Take no notice of him. Did anything happen after that?" one of us asked.

"Yes. So I went on dancing with her and didn't notice the time passing. The musicians struck up the same old mazurka tune over and over again with the sort of despairing weariness you often see at the end of a ball—you know the kind of thing—and in the drawing-room the mamas and papas had already got up from their card tables ready for supper. The servants were more frequently hurrying through the room with various things. It was after two o'clock. I had to take advantage of these last minutes. I asked her to dance again, and for the hundredth time we glided down the room.

" 'So, is the quadrille after supper mine?' I said to her, taking her back to her place.

" 'Of course,' she said smiling, 'unless I have to go.'

" 'I won't let that happen,' I said.

" 'Give me my fan a moment,' she said.

" 'I'm reluctant to part with it,' I said, handing her the cheap little white fan.

" 'Well here you are then, so that you don't grieve,' she said, and she plucked a little feather from the fan and gave it to me. I took the feather, and only my eyes were able to express the rapturous gratitude I felt inside. I was not only cheerful and contented, I was happy, I was blissful, I was good, I was not myself, but some otherworldly being, ignorant of evil and capable only of good. I concealed the feather in my glove, and stood up, not having the strength to walk away from her.

" 'Look, they're asking papa to dance,' she said to me, pointing to the tall, imposing figure of her father, a colonel with silver epaulettes on his jacket, who was standing in the doorway with our hostess and some other women.

"The loud voice of our hostess with her diamond frontlet and her shoulders like the Empress Elizabeth's called over in our direction, 'Varenka, come here.' Varenka went over to the door, and I followed her. '*Ma chère,* do persuade your father to take the floor with you. Now please, Pyotr Vladislavich,' said our hostess, turning to the colonel.

"Varenka's father was a very handsome, elderly man, tall, stately, and well preserved. He had a ruddy face, a white upswept moustache *à la* Nicholas I, white whiskers which came to meet the moustache, and hair combed forward over his temples; and the same tender, merry smile as radiated from his daughter sparkled in his eyes and on his lips. He was superbly built, with a broad chest protruding in military fashion and modestly decorated with medals. His shoulders were strong and his legs long and slender. He was a military commander with the highly disciplined manner of an old campaigner under Nicholas.

"When we approached him the colonel tried to refuse, saying that he had forgotten how to dance, but eventually he smiled, swung his right arm to the left, and took his sword out of its sheath and handed it to an obliging young man standing near by. Then, pulling a suede glove onto his right hand, he said with a smile, 'Everything according to the rules,' took his daughter's hand and stood one quarter turned, waiting for the music.

"When the mazurka began he tapped one foot with gusto and struck out with the other, his tall, solid figure moving first of all gently, then noisily and spiritedly about the room, his soles stamping on the floor and his feet clicking together.

Varenka's graceful figure glided beside him almost unnoticed as she shortened or lengthened the steps of her little white satin feet at just the right moment. The whole room followed their every movement. For myself I not only admired them, but felt an ecstatic tenderness as I watched them. I was especially moved by his boots with footstraps round them—they were fine calfskin boots, not the latest pointed type, but old-fashioned, with square toes and without heels. Obviously they had been made for him by the regimental cobbler. 'He doesn't buy fashionable boots, but wears homemade ones,' I thought. 'That's so he can bring his favorite daughter out in society and buy clothes for her.' And I found the square toes of his boots particularly touching. One could see that at one time he had been a superb dancer, but now he was heavy, and his legs had not sufficient spring for all those elegant and rapid steps he tried to execute. Nevertheless he still managed two circles round the room with agility. And on one occasion, when he quickly brought his legs together and—even though somewhat heavily—went down onto one knee, while she, smiling and straightening her skirt, glided smoothly around him, there was a loud burst of applause from everyone in the room. Raising himself with some effort, he gently and tenderly drew his daughter's face towards him and kissed her forehead, then he brought her over to me, thinking that I was dancing with her. I said that I was not her partner. 'Well, never mind, you dance with her now,' he said, smiling affectionately and replacing his sword in its sheath.

"Just as once one drop has been poured from a bottle its whole content bursts forth, in a great stream, so in my heart my love for Varenka released all that heart's latent capacity for love. At that moment I embraced the whole world with my love. I loved the hostess with her diamond frontlet and her Elizabethan neckline, and her husband and her guests and her servants and even Anisimov, the engineer, who was sulking because of me. And looking at her father, with his homemade boots and his tender smile—the same smile that Varenka had—I experienced an emotion of rapturous affection.

"The mazurka ended, and the hosts asked their guests in to supper, but Colonel B. declined, saying that he had to get up early next morning, and took his leave of the host and his wife. I was afraid he might take her away too, but she stayed with her mother.

"After supper I danced the promised quadrille with her and, even though I seemed to be infinitely happy, my happiness continued to grow. We said nothing of love. I asked neither her nor even myself whether she loved me. It was enough for me to love her. And I was afraid of only one thing—that something might spoil my happiness.

"When I arrived home, undressed, and began to think of sleep, I realized that that was quite impossible. In my hand I held the little feather from her fan and also one of her gloves which she had given me as she was leaving, when I had helped first her mother and then her into their carriage. I looked at these things, and without closing my eyes I could see her again before me. I saw her faced with a choice between two partners and trying to guess aright where I would be standing in the set; I saw her saying in her lovely voice, 'Pride? That's it, isn't it?' and joyfully giving me her hand; I saw her at supper lifting a glass of champagne to her lips and looking at me shyly with her soft eyes. But most vividly of all I saw her partnering her father, dancing smoothly round him and, with pride and delight for both her father and herself, looking at the admiring crowd around her. And I couldn't help uniting the two of them in a single overwhelming feeling of affection.

"At that time I was living with my late brother. In general my brother didn't like society and didn't go to balls, and now he was working for his examinations at the university and leading a highly proper life. He was asleep. I looked at his face, buried in the pillow and half-covered by a flannel blanket, and I felt lovingly sorry for him, sorry that he didn't know and couldn't share the happiness I was experiencing. Our servant Petrushka came to meet me with a candle and wanted to help me undress, but I sent him away. The sight of his sleepy face and his disheveled hair seemed to me intensely moving. Trying not to make a noise, I went on tiptoe to my room and sat down on the bed. No, I was too happy, I couldn't sleep. On top of that I was hot in our heated rooms and, without taking off my uniform, I crept quietly into the hall, put on my overcoat, opened the outside door, and went into the street.

"I had left the ball between four and five o'clock, then I had come home and sat there for a while, so that about two more hours had gone by, and when I went out it was already light. The weather was typical for that time of year. There was a fog, and slushy snow was melting on the paths and dripping from every roof. At that time Varenka's family was living at the far end of the town, just past a large open space, on one side of which there was a parade ground and on the other a girls' boarding school. I went along our deserted side street and out on to the main road, where pedestrians and carters with firewood on their sledges were beginning to appear. As the sledges moved, their runners grated against the surface of the road. The horses, rhythmically nodding their damp heads beneath their gleaming harnesses, and the draymen, splashing along in huge boots beside their carts, their shoulders covered with bast mats, and the houses along the road, which in the fog seemed to be towering above me—all these things I found especially pleasing and significant.

"As I came to the open space where their house stood, I could see at the other end of it, in the direction of the parade ground, some large black object, and from the same direction came the sound of pipe and drum. My heart still sang, and now and again I could still hear the tune of the mazurka. But this was some other kind of music, cruel and harsh. 'What on earth can that be?' I thought, and set off along the slippery path running through the middle of the open space in the direction of the noise. I had gone only a hundred yards or so when through the fog I was able to make out a large number of black figures. They were obviously soldiers. 'That's it, they're out training,' I thought and, together with a blacksmith in a short, greasy fur coat and an apron who was walking in front of me carrying something, I went closer. Soldiers in black uniforms were standing in two lines opposite each other, all with their rifles at ease, and motionless. Behind them stood a drummer and a piper, incessantly playing the same shrill unpleasant tune. 'What's that they're doing?' I asked the blacksmith, who had stopped alongside me. 'They're making the Tatar run the gauntlet for trying to desert,' answered the blacksmith angrily, as he looked to the far end of the lines.

"I began to look in that direction too and caught sight of something terrible coming towards me between the two rows of soldiers. What was coming towards me was a man stripped to the waist and bound to the soldiers who were leading him forward. Alongside him was a tall officer in a greatcoat and a peaked cap, a figure who seemed familiar to me. With blows being showered upon him from both sides and dragging his feet through the slushy snow, the prisoner was moving towards me, his whole body twitching; sometimes he would fall backwards, whereupon the corporals who were leading him on with their rifles would push him forwards; and sometimes he would lurch forwards, whereupon they would pull him up and stop him falling over. And all the time the tall resolute officer strode firmly beside him. It was her father, with his ruddy face, white moustache, and whiskers.

"Every time he was hit the prisoner screwed up his face with pain and turned it, as if in surprise, to the side from which the blow came, and gritting his white teeth, he repeated over and over again the same words. Only when he drew quite close to me could I hear these words. He sobbed rather than spoke them: 'Brothers, have mercy; brothers, have mercy.' But his brothers had no mercy, and when the column drew level with me, I saw the soldier standing opposite me take a resolute step forward and, swishing his stick through the air, bring it down hard across the Tatar's back. The Tatar lurched forwards, but the corporals held him up, and a similar blow fell upon him from the other side, and then again from my side, and then again from the other side. The colonel strode alongside, looking now at his feet, now at the prisoner, inhaling deeply, as he blew out his cheeks and then slowly releasing the air through his pursed lips. Once the column had passed where I was standing I caught a glimpse through the ranks of the prisoner's back. It was something so bloody, so glaringly red and unreal, I couldn't believe it was the body of a man. 'Lord forgive them,' said the blacksmith alongside me out loud.

"The column disappeared into the distance, and all the time they continued to beat the stumbling, writhing man from both sides, and all the time the drum and the pipe went on playing, and the tall, imposing figure of the colonel strode with the same resolute step alongside the prisoner. Suddenly the colonel stopped and went quickly up to one of the soldiers. 'I'll teach you to be soft,' I heard his angry voice shout. 'So you're going to pat him like that, are you?' And I saw him with his strong, gloved fist punch a frightened, undersized, puny soldier in the face because he was not bringing his stick down hard enough on the red back of the Tatar. 'Bring fresh rods!' he shouted, looking round, and caught sight of me. Pretending he didn't know me, he turned away hastily, with a menacing, ill-tempered frown on his face. I was so ashamed I didn't know where to look; it was as if I had been caught committing the most despicable crime, and I lowered my eyes and hurried home. The roll of the drum and the whistling of the pipe rang in my ears the whole way, and I could hear the words, 'Brothers, have mercy,' and then the self-assured and angry voice of the colonel crying, 'So you're going to be soft with him, are you?' And in the meantime my heart had become so full with an almost physical anguish, bordering on nausea, that I stopped still several times, and it seemed as if my stomach were about to heave and purge itself of all the horror which had entered into me at that sight. I don't remember how I got home and into my bed. But, as soon as I started to fall asleep, I began to see and hear everything again and leapt up. 'Obviously he knows something that I don't,' I said to myself, thinking of the colonel. 'If I knew what he knows, I would understand what I saw and it wouldn't torment me.' But, however much I thought, I couldn't grasp what the colonel knew, and when eventually, towards evening, I fell asleep, it was only after I had visited a friend and drunk myself silly with him.

"Well, do you think I decided there and then that what I had seen was evil? Not at all. 'If it was done with such certainty, and was recognized by everyone as being inevitable, then it follows they must have known something I didn't,' I kept thinking, and tried to realize what that something was. But, hard as I tried, I couldn't understand. And without this understanding I was unable to go into the army, as I had wanted to do previously, and not only did I not serve as a soldier, I didn't take up a government position at all and, as you can see, I haven't made anything of my life."

"Oh, come, we know all about your not having made anything of your life," said one of us. "How many other people would have made nothing of their lives, if it hadn't been for you. That's what you really ought to say."

"Really! That's quite ridiculous," said Ivan Vasilevich with genuine annoyance.

"And what about your love?" we asked.

"Love? My love began to wane that very day. Whenever she fell into a thoughtful mood—and that used to happen quite a lot—a smile would appear on her face, and I would immediately recall the colonel on the parade ground and feel somehow awkward and uncomfortable; I stopped meeting her so often and my love just faded away. You see then what can happen, and how a man's entire life can be changed and redirected. And yet you say . . ." he concluded.

Interpretive Questions

1. Why is Ivan's love for Varenka so closely tied to his feelings about her father?
2. Is the narrator correct in saying that Ivan forgot the point of his story?
3. Why does Ivan try to deny that what he saw on the parade ground was evil?
4. Why does the Colonel fail to do "everything according to the rules" at the ball? Does he do everything according to the rules at the parade ground?
5. Was Ivan's life ruined by the incident at the parade ground?

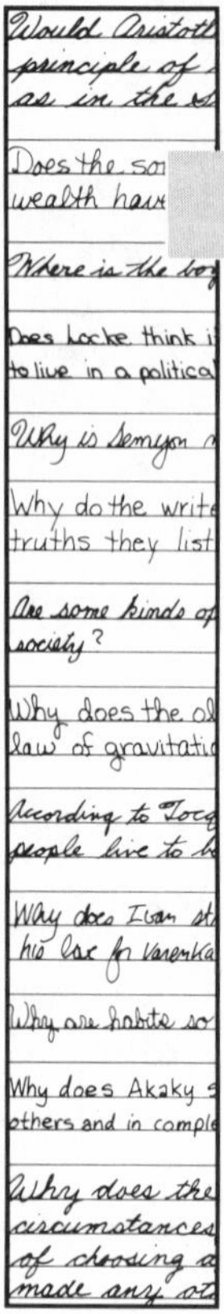

PRACTICE

Writing Interpretive Questions

"After the Ball"

A reader made notes from a passage in "After the Ball," then developed some of them into interpretive questions.

"The column disappeared into the distance, and all the time they continued to beat the stumbling, writhing man from both sides, and all the time the drum and the pipe went on playing, and the tall, imposing figure of the colonel strode with the same resolute step alongside the prisoner. Suddenly the colonel stopped and went quickly up to one of the soldiers. 'I'll teach you to be soft,' I heard his angry voice shout. 'So you're going to pat him like that, are you?' And I saw him

music again

like a dance partner

with his strong, gloved fist punch a frightened,	again– attention to Colonel's gloves
undersized, puny soldier in the face because he	cruelty?
was not bringing his stick down hard enough	or duty?
on the red back of the Tatar. 'Bring fresh rods!'	a foreigner
he shouted, looking round, and caught sight of	
me. Pretending he didn't know me, he turned	why?
away hastily, with a menacing, ill-tempered	
frown on his face . . . ."	

1. Why does the author have music play while the Tatar is beaten?
2. Why does Ivan notice the Colonel's gloves both at the ball and at the parade ground?
3. Does the Colonel punch one of his soldiers because he is cruel or because he wants to do his duty?
4. Why does the Colonel pretend not to know Ivan?

Using the example you have just read as a guide, make your own notes on the following passage, then turn those notes into interpretive questions.

> . . . I was so ashamed I didn't know where to look; it was as if I had been caught committing the most despicable crime, and I lowered my eyes and hurried home. The roll of the drum and the whistling of

the pipe rang in my ears the whole way, and I could hear the words, 'Brothers, have mercy,' and then the self-assured and angry voice of the colonel crying, 'So you're going to be soft with him, are you?' And in the meantime my heart had become so full with an almost physical anguish, bordering on nausea, that I stopped still several times, and it seemed as if my stomach were about to heave and purge itself of all the horror which had entered into me at that sight. I don't remember how I got home and into my bed. But, as soon as I started to fall asleep, I began to see and hear everything again and leapt up. 'Obviously he knows something that I don't,' I said to myself, thinking of the colonel. 'If I knew what he knows, I would understand what I saw, and it wouldn't torment me.' But, however much I thought, I couldn't grasp what the colonel knew, and when eventually, towards evening, I fell asleep, it was only after I had visited a friend and drunk myself silly with him.

XI

By and About William James

(1842–1910)

William James, the distinguished American psychologist and philosopher, was the elder brother of novelist Henry James.

On the need to risk ourselves:

> So far as man stands for anything, and is productive or originative at all, his entire vital function may be said to have to deal with maybes. Not a victory is gained, not a deed of faithfulness or courage is done, except upon a maybe; not a service, not a sally of generosity, not a scientific exploration or experiment or text-book that may not be a mistake. It is only by risking our persons from one hour to another that we live at all. And often enough our faith beforehand in an uncertified result *is the only thing that makes the result come true.*

On point of view:

> We can act *as if* there were a God; feel *as if* we were free; consider Nature *as if* she were full of special designs; lay plans *as if* we were to be immortal; and we find then that these words do make a genuine difference in our moral life.

On conviction:

> I cannot understand the willingness to act, no matter how we feel, without the belief that acts are really good and bad. I cannot understand the belief that an act is bad, without regret at its happening. I cannot understand regret without the admission of real, genuine possibilities in the world. Only *then* is it other than a mockery to feel, after we have failed to do our best, that an irreparable opportunity is gone from the universe, the loss of which it must forever after mourn.

Habit

William James

Practical Effects of Habit

First, habit simplifies our movements, makes them accurate, and diminishes fatigue.

Man is born with a tendency to do more things than he has ready-made arrangements for in his nerve centers. Most of the performances of other animals are automatic. But in him the number of them is so enormous that most of them must be the fruit of painful study. If practice did not make perfect, nor habit economize the expense of nervous and muscular energy, he would be in a sorry plight. As Dr. Maudsley says:

> If an act became no easier after being done several times, if the careful direction of consciousness were necessary to its accomplishment on each occasion, it is evident that the whole activity of a lifetime might be confined to one or two deeds—that no progress could take place in development. A man might be occupied all day in dressing and undressing himself; the attitude of his body would absorb all his attention and energy; the washing of his hands or the fastening of a button would be as difficult to him on

---

*A selection from *Psychology: Briefer Course*.

> each occasion as to the child on its first trial; and he would, furthermore, be completely exhausted by his exertions. Think of the pains necessary to teach a child to stand, of the many efforts which it must make, and of the ease with which it at last stands, unconscious of any effort. . . .

Secondly, *habit diminishes the conscious attention with which our acts are performed.*

One may state this abstractly thus: If an act require for its execution a chain, *A, B, C, D, E, F, G,* etc., of successive nervous events, then in the first performances of the action the conscious will must choose each of these events from a number of wrong alternatives that tend to present themselves; but habit soon brings it about that each event calls up its own appropriate successor without any alternative offering itself, and without any reference to the conscious will, until at last the whole chain, *A, B, C, D, E, F, G,* rattles itself off as soon as *A* occurs, just as if *A* and the rest of the chain were fused into a continuous stream. Whilst we are learning to walk, to ride, to swim, skate, fence, write, play, or sing, we interrupt ourselves at every step by unnecessary movements and false notes. When we are proficients, on the contrary, the results follow not only with the very minimum of muscular action requisite to bring them forth, but they follow from a single instantaneous "cue." The marksman sees the bird, and, before he knows it, he has aimed and shot. A gleam in his adversary's eye, a momentary pressure from his rapier, and the fencer finds that he has instantly made the right parry and return. A glance at the musical hieroglyphics, and the pianist's fingers have rippled through a shower of notes. And not only is it the right thing at the right time that we thus involuntarily do, but the wrong thing also, if it be an habitual thing. . . . We all have a definite routine manner of performing certain daily offices connected with the toilet, with the opening and shutting of familiar cupboards, and the like. But our higher thought centers know hardly anything about the matter. Few men can tell offhand which sock, shoe, or trousers leg they put on first. They must first mentally rehearse the act; and even that is often insufficient—the act must be *performed.* So of the questions, Which valve of the shutters opens first? Which way does my door swing? etc. I cannot *tell* the answer; yet my *hand* never makes a mistake. No one can *describe* the order in which he brushes his hair or teeth; yet it is likely that the order is a pretty fixed one in all of us.

These results may be expressed as follows:

In action grown habitual, what instigates each new muscular contraction to take place in its appointed order is not a thought or a perception, but the *sensation occasioned by the muscular contraction just finished.* A strictly voluntary act has to be guided by idea, perception, and volition, throughout its whole course. In habitual action, mere sensation is a sufficient guide, and the upper regions of brain and mind are set comparatively free. A diagram will make the matter clear:

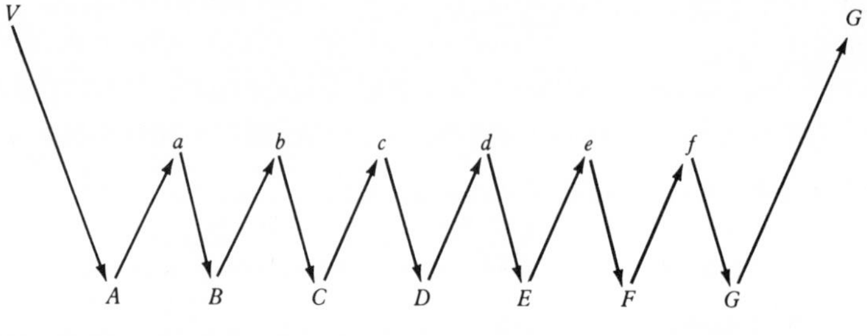

Let *A, B, C, D, E, F, G* represent an habitual chain of muscular contractions, and let *a, b, c, d, e, f* stand for the several sensations which these contractions excite in us when they are successively performed. Such sensations will usually be in the parts moved, but they may also be effects of the movement upon the eye or the ear. Through them, and through them alone, we are made aware whether or not the contraction has occurred. When the series, *A, B, C, D, E, F, G,* is being learned, each of these sensations becomes the object of a separate act of attention by the mind. We test each movement intellectually, to see if it has been rightly performed, before advancing to the next. We hesitate, compare, choose, revoke, reject, etc.; and the order by which the next movement is discharged is an express order from the ideational centers after this deliberation has been gone through.

In habitual action, on the contrary, the only impulse which the intellectual centers need send down is that which carries the command to *start.* This is represented in the diagram by *V;* it may be a thought of the first movement or of the last result, or a mere perception of some of the habitual conditions of the chain, the presence, e.g., of the keyboard near the hand. In the present example, no sooner has this conscious thought or volition instigated movement *A,* than *A,* through the sensation *a* of its own occurrence, awakens *B* reflexly; *B* then excites *C* through *b,* and so on till the chain is ended, when the intellect generally takes cognizance of the final result. The intellectual perception at the end is indicated in the diagram by the sensible effect of the movement *G* being represented at *G′*, in the ideational centers above the merely sensational line. The sensational impressions, *a, b, c, d, e, f,* are all supposed to have their seat below the ideational level.

Habits depend on sensations not attended to. We have called *a, b, c, d, e, f,* by the name of "sensations." If sensations, they are sensations to which we are usually inattentive; but that they are more than unconscious nerve currents seems certain, for they catch our attention if they go wrong. Schneider's account of these sensations deserves to be quoted.

> In the act of walking, even when our attention is entirely absorbed elsewhere, it is doubtful whether we could preserve equilibrium if no sensation of our body's attitude were there, and doubtful whether we should advance our leg if we had no sensation of its movement

> as executed, and not even a minimal feeling of impulse to set it down. Knitting appears altogether mechanical, and the knitter keeps up her knitting even while she reads or is engaged in lively talk. But if we ask her how this is possible, she will hardly reply that the knitting goes on of itself. She will rather say that she has a feeling of it, that she feels in her hands that she knits and how she must knit, and that therefore the movements of knitting are called forth and regulated by the sensations associated therewithal, even when the attention is called away. . . .

Again:

> When a pupil begins to play on the violin, to keep him from raising his right elbow in playing a book is placed under his right armpit, which he is ordered to hold fast by keeping the upper arm tight against his body. The muscular feelings, and feelings of contact connected with the book, provoke an impulse to press it tight. But often it happens that the beginner, whose attention gets absorbed in the production of the notes, lets drop the book. Later, however, this never happens; the faintest sensations of contact suffice to awaken the impulse to keep it in its place, and the attention may be wholly absorbed by the notes and the fingering with the left hand. *The simultaneous combination of movements is thus in the first instance conditioned by the facility with which in us, alongside of intellectual processes, processes of inattentive feeling may still go on.*

Ethical and Pedagogical Importance of the Principle of Habit

"Habit a second nature! Habit is ten times nature," the Duke of Wellington is said to have exclaimed; and the degree to which this is true no one probably can appreciate as well as one who is a veteran soldier himself. The daily drill and the years of discipline end by fashioning a man completely over again, as to most of the possibilities of his conduct.

"There is a story," says Prof. Huxley, "which is credible enough, though it may not be true, of a practical joker who, seeing a discharged veteran carrying home his dinner, suddenly called out, 'Attention!' whereupon the man instantly brought his hands down, and lost his mutton and potatoes in the gutter. The drill had been thorough, and its effects had become embodied in the man's nervous structure."

Riderless cavalry horses, at many a battle, have been seen to come together and go through their customary evolutions at the sound of the bugle call. Most domestic beasts seem machines almost pure and simple, undoubtingly, unhesitatingly doing from minute to minute the duties they have been taught, and giving no sign that the possibility of an alternative ever suggests itself to their mind. Men grown old in prison have asked to be readmitted after being once set free. In a railroad accident a menagerie tiger, whose cage had broken open, is said to have emerged, but presently crept back again, as if too much bewildered by his new responsibilities, so that he was without difficulty secured.

Habit is thus the enormous flywheel of society, its most precious conservative agent. It alone is what keeps us all within the bounds of ordinance, and saves the children of fortune from the envious uprisings of the poor. It alone prevents the hardest and most repulsive walks of life from being deserted by those brought up to tread therein. It keeps the fisherman and the deckhand at sea through the winter; it holds the miner in his darkness, and nails the countryman to his log cabin and his lonely farm through all the months of snow; it protects us from invasion by the natives of the desert and the frozen zone. It dooms us all to fight out the battle of life upon the lines of our nurture or our early choice, and to make the best of a pursuit that disagrees, because there is no other for which we are fitted, and it is too late to begin again. It keeps different social strata from mixing. Already at the age of twenty-five you see the professional mannerism settling down on the young commercial traveler, on the young doctor, on the young minister, on the young counselor-at-law. You see the little lines of cleavage running through the character, the tricks of thought, the prejudices, the ways of the "shop," in a word, from which the man can by-and-by no more escape than his coat sleeve can suddenly fall into a new set of folds. On the whole, it is best he should not escape. It is well for the world that in most of us, by the age of thirty, the character has set like plaster, and will never soften again.

If the period between twenty and thirty is the critical one in the formation of intellectual and professional habits, the period below twenty is more important still for the fixing of *personal* habits, properly so called, such as vocalization and pronunciation, gesture, motion, and address. Hardly ever is a language learned after twenty spoken without a foreign accent; hardly ever can a youth transferred to the society of his betters unlearn the nasality and other vices of speech bred in him by the associations of his growing years. Hardly ever, indeed, no matter how much money there be in his pocket, can he even learn to *dress* like a gentleman-born. The merchants offer their wares as eagerly to him as to the veriest "swell," but he simply *cannot* buy the right things. An invisible law, as strong as gravitation, keeps him within his orbit, arrayed this year as he was the last; and how his better-clad acquaintances contrive to get the things they wear will be for him a mystery till his dying day.

The great thing, then, in all education, is to *make our nervous system our ally instead of our enemy.* It is to fund and capitalize our acquisitions, and live at ease upon the interest of the fund. *For this we must make automatic and habitual, as early as possible, as many useful actions as we can,* and guard against the growing into ways that are likely to be disadvantageous to us, as we should guard against the plague. The more of the details of our daily life we can hand over to the effortless custody of automatism, the more our higher powers of mind will be set free for their own proper work. There is no more miserable human being than one in whom nothing is habitual but indecision, and for whom the lighting of every cigar, the drinking of every cup, the time of rising and going to bed every day, and the beginning of every bit of work, are subjects of express volitional deliberation. Full half the time of such a man goes to the deciding, or regretting, of matters which ought to be so ingrained in him as practically not to exist for his consciousness at all. If there be such daily duties not yet ingrained in any one of my readers, let him begin this very hour to set the matter right.

In Professor Bain's chapter on "The Moral Habits" there are some admirable practical remarks laid down. Two great maxims emerge from his treatment. The first is that in the acquisition of a new habit, or the leaving off of an old one, we must take care to *launch ourselves with as strong and decided an initiative as possible.* Accumulate all the possible circumstances which shall reinforce the right motives; put yourself assiduously in conditions that encourage the new way; make engagements incompatible with the old; take a public pledge, if the case allows; in short, envelop your resolution with every aid you know. This will give your new beginning such a momentum that the temptation to break down will not occur as soon as it otherwise might; and every day during which a breakdown is postponed adds to the chances of its not occurring at all.

The second maxim is: *Never suffer an exception to occur till the new habit is securely rooted in your life.* Each lapse is like the letting fall of a ball of string which one is carefully winding up; a single slip undoes more than a great many turns will wind again. *Continuity* of training is the great means of making the nervous system act infallibly right. As Professor Bain says:

> The peculiarity of the moral habits, contradistinguishing them from the intellectual acquisitions, is the presence of two hostile powers, one to be gradually raised into the ascendant over the other. It is necessary, above all things, in such a situation, never to lose a battle. Every gain on the wrong side undoes the effect of many conquests on the right. The essential precaution, therefore, is so to regulate the two opposing powers that the one may have a series of uninterrupted successes, until repetition has fortified it to such a degree as to enable it to cope with the opposition, under any circumstances. This is the theoretically best career of mental progress.

The need of securing success at the *outset* is imperative. Failure at first is apt to damp the energy of all future attempts, whereas past experiences of success nerve one to future vigor. Goethe says to a man who consulted him about an enterprise but mistrusted his own powers: "Ach! you need only blow on your hands!" And the remark illustrates the effect on Goethe's spirits of his own habitually successful career.

The question of "tapering off," in abandoning such habits as drink and opium indulgence comes in here, and is a question about which experts differ within certain limits, and in regard to what may be best for an individual case. In the main, however, all expert opinion would agree that abrupt acquisition of the new habit is the best way, *if there be a real possibility of carrying it out.* We must be careful not to give the will so stiff a task as to insure its defeat at the very outset; but, *provided one can stand it,* a sharp period of suffering, and then a free time, is the best thing to aim at, whether in giving up a habit like that of opium, or in simply changing one's hours of rising or of work. It is surprising how soon a desire will die of inanition if it be *never* fed.

> One must first learn, unmoved, looking neither to the right nor left, to walk firmly on the straight and narrow path, before one can begin "to make one's self over again." He who every day makes a fresh resolve is like one who, arriving at the edge of the ditch he is to leap, forever stops and returns for a fresh run. Without *unbroken* advance there is no such thing as *accumulation* of the ethical forces possible, and to make this possible, and to exercise us and habituate us in it, is the sovereign blessing of regular work.*

A third maxim may be added to the preceding pair: *Seize the very first possible opportunity to act on every resolution you make, and on every emotional prompting you may experience in the direction of the habits you aspire to gain.* It is not in the moment of their forming, but in the moment of their producing *motor effects,* that resolves and aspirations communicate the new "set" to the brain. As the author last quoted remarks:

> The actual presence of the practical opportunity alone furnishes the fulcrum upon which the lever can rest, by means of which the moral will may multiply its strength, and raise itself aloft. He who has no solid ground to press against will never get beyond the stage of empty gesture-making.

No matter how full a reservoir of *maxims* one may possess, and no matter how good one's *sentiments* may be, if one have not taken advantage of every concrete opportunity to *act,* one's character may remain entirely unaffected for the better. With mere good intentions, hell is proverbially paved. And this is an obvious consequence of the principles we have laid down. A "character," as J. S. Mill says, "is a completely fashioned will"; and a will, in the sense in which he means it, is an aggregate of tendencies to act in a firm and prompt and definite way upon all the principal emergencies of life. A tendency to act only becomes effectively ingrained in us in proportion to the

---

* J. Bahnsen: 'Beiträge zu Charakterologie' (1867), vol. I, p. 209.

uninterrupted frequency with which the actions actually occur, and the brain "grows" to their use. When a resolve or a fine glow of feeling is allowed to evaporate without bearing practical fruit it is worse than a chance lost; it works so as positively to hinder future resolutions and emotions from taking the normal path of discharge. There is no more contemptible type of human character than that of the nerveless sentimentalist and dreamer, who spends his life in a weltering sea of sensibility and emotion, but who never does a manly concrete deed. Rousseau, inflaming all the mothers of France, by his eloquence, to follow Nature and nurse their babies themselves, while he sends his own children to the foundling hospital, is the classical example of what I mean. But every one of us in his measure, whenever, after glowing for an abstractly formulated Good, he practically ignores some actual case among the squalid "other particulars" of which that same Good lurks disguised, treads straight on Rousseau's path. All Goods are disguised by the vulgarity of their concomitants, in this work-a-day world; but woe to him who can only recognize them when he thinks them in their pure and abstract form! The habit of excessive novel-reading and theater-going will produce true monsters in this line. The weeping of the Russian lady over the fictitious personages in the play, while her coachman is freezing to death on his seat outside, is the sort of thing that everywhere happens on a less glaring scale. Even the habit of excessive indulgence in music, for those who are neither performers themselves nor musically gifted enough to take it in a purely intellectual way, has probably a relaxing effect upon the character. One becomes filled with emotions which habitually pass without prompting to any deed, and so the inertly sentimental condition is kept up. The remedy would be, never to suffer one's self to have an emotion at a concert without expressing it afterward in *some* active way. Let the expression be the least thing in the world—speaking genially to one's grandmother, or giving up one's seat in a horse-car, if nothing more heroic offers—but let it not fail to take place.

These latter cases make us aware that it is not simply *particular lines* of discharge, but also *general forms* of discharge, that seem to be grooved out by habit in the brain. Just as, if we let our emotions evaporate, they get into a way of evaporating; so there is reason to suppose that if we often flinch from making an effort, before we know it the effort-making capacity will be gone; and that, if we suffer the wandering of our attention, presently it will wander all the time. Attention and effort are, as we shall see later, but two names for the same psychic fact. To what brain processes they correspond we do not know. The strongest reason for believing that they do depend on brain processes at all, and are not pure acts of the spirit, is just this fact, that they seem in some degree subject to the law of habit, which is a material law. As a final practical maxim, relative to these habits of the will, we may, then, offer something like this: *Keep the faculty of effort alive in you by a little gratuitous exercise every day.* That is, be systematically ascetic or heroic in little unnecessary points, do every day or two something for no other reason than that you would rather not do it, so that when the hour of dire need draws nigh, it may find you not unnerved and untrained to stand the test. Ascetism of this sort is like the insurance which a man pays on his house and goods. The tax does him no good at the time, and possibly may never bring him a return. But if the fire *does* come, his having paid it will be his salvation from ruin. So with the man who has daily inured himself to habits of concentrated attention, energetic volition, and self-denial in unnecessary things. He will stand like a tower when everything rocks around him, and when his softer fellow mortals are winnowed like chaff in the blast.

The physiological study of mental conditions is thus the

most powerful ally of hortatory ethics. The hell to be endured hereafter, of which theology tells, is no worse than the hell we make for ourselves in this world by habitually fashioning our characters in the wrong way. Could the young but realize how soon they will become mere walking bundles of habits, they would give more heed to their conduct while in the plastic state. We are spinning our own fates, good or evil, and never to be undone. Every smallest stroke of virtue or of vice leaves its never so little scar. The drunken Rip Van Winkle, in Jefferson's play, excuses himself for every fresh dereliction by saying, "I won't count this time!" Well! he may not count it, and a kind Heaven may not count it; but it is being counted none the less. Down among his nerve cells and fibers the molecules are counting it, registering and storing it up to be used against him when the next temptation comes. Nothing we ever do is, in strict scientific literalness, wiped out. Of course this has its good side as well as its bad one. As we become permanent drunkards by so many separate drinks, so we become saints in the moral, and authorities and experts in the practical and scientific spheres, by so many separate acts and hours of work. Let no youth have any anxiety about the upshot of his education, whatever the line of it may be. If he keep faithfully busy each hour of the working day, he may safely leave the final result to itself. He can with perfect certainty count on waking up some fine morning, to find himself one of the competent ones of his generation in whatever pursuit he may have singled out. Silently, between all the details of his business, the *power of judging* in all that class of matter will have built itself up within him as a possession that will never pass away. Young people should know this truth in advance. The ignorance of it has probably engendered more discouragement and faintheartedness in youths embarking on arduous careers than all other causes put together.

Interpretive Questions

1. What does James mean by a "moral habit"?
2. According to James, is it always possible for a person to change his character?
3. Why does the "power of judging" increase in a youth who develops good habits?
4. Why does James warn us about thinking of Goods "in their pure and abstract form"?
5. Does James suggest that obtaining a good education is mostly a matter of forming certain habits?

XII

By and About Nikolai Gogol

(1809–1852)

Nikolai Vasilievich Gogol was the first of the great Russian novelists. Turgenev once remarked that to the Russians of his generation, "Gogol was more than a writer: he revealed us to ourselves." Dostoyevsky would later claim that all Russian realists had come "from under Gogol's overcoat."

Gogol insists on the reality of his strange characters:

> I never created anything out of mere imagination. Only in those things was I successful which I took from reality and which were based on the data I knew. I could fathom a man, then, only when I had seen all the minutest details of his exterior. Yet I never *painted* a portrait by simply copying it. I *created* portraits, but I created them on the ground of consideration rather than on that of mere imagination. The more details I had seen and considered, the better were my productions.

Although his heroes are "not at all villains," Gogol once explained:

> [Their] banality frightened my readers. What frightened them is that my heroes follow one after the other, one more banal than the other, that there is not one consoling scene, that there is nowhere for the poor reader to rest and take a breath, and, after having read the whole book, it seems exactly as though he were emerging from some stifling cellar into God's light. . . . The Russian is more frightened of his insignificance than of all his vices and shortcomings.

In writing *Dead Souls* he realized "how frightening . . . it can be to a man when he is presented with shadows, and how much more threatening is *the absence of light*." But laughter, Gogol claims, brings light:

> No one has come forward in defense of laughter. I am a comic author, I have served it honestly, and thus I must be its defender. No, laughter is more meaningful and more profound than is thought. Not the laughter engendered by momentary irritation,

by a bilious sickly disposition of character; and not the light laughter that serves people as idle entertainment and pastime; but the laughter that flies out of the luminous nature of man, that flies from it because in its depths is enclosed his eternally gushing spring, that deepens the subject, compelling whatever would slip by to come forth clearly, and without whose penetrating power the pettiness and emptiness of life would not frighten mankind so much. The contemptible and the worthless past that he indifferently walks by each day would not grow before him with such terrible, almost ridiculous power, and he would not, shuddering, cry, "Are there really such people?" when, as he well knows, there are worse people. No, those who say that laughter incites are unjust. Only the dismal incites, while laughter gives light. Many things would incite man if presented in their nakedness; but illuminated by the power of laughter, they bring reconciliation to the soul.

The Overcoat

Nikolai Gogol

Once, in a department ... but better not mention which department. There is nothing touchier than departments, regiments, bureaus, in fact, any caste of officials. Things have reached the point where every individual takes an insult to himself as a slur on society as a whole. It seems that not long ago a complaint was lodged by the police inspector of I forget which town, in which he stated clearly that government institutions had been imperiled and his own sacred name taken in vain. In evidence he produced a huge volume, practically a novel, in which, every ten pages, a police inspector appears, and what's more, at times completely drunk. So, to stay out of trouble, let us refer to it just as *a department.*

And so, once, in *a department,* there worked a clerk. This clerk was nothing much to speak of: he was small, somewhat pockmarked, his hair was somewhat reddish and he even looked somewhat blind. Moreover, he was getting thin on top, had wrinkled cheeks and a complexion that might be aptly described as hemorrhoidal. But that's the Petersburg climate for you.

As to his civil-service category (for first a man's standing should be established), he was what is called an eternal pen-pusher, a lowly ninth-class clerk, the usual butt of the jeers and jokes of those writers who have the congenial habit of biting those who cannot bite back.

The clerk's name was Shoenik. There is no doubt that this name derives from shoe, but we know nothing of how, why, or when. His father, his grandfather, and even his brother-in-law wore boots, having new soles put on them not more than three times a year.

His first name was Akaky, like his father's, which made him Akaky Akakievich. This may sound somewhat strange and contrived but it is not contrived at all, and, in view of the circumstances, any other name was unthinkable. If I am not mistaken, Akaky Akakievich was born on the night between the 22nd and the 23rd of March. His late mother, an excellent woman and the wife of a clerk, had made all the arrangements for the child's christening, and, while she was still confined to her bed, the godparents arrived: the worthy Ivan Yeroshkin, head clerk in the Senate, and Arina Whitetumkin, the wife of a police captain, a woman of rare virtue.

The new mother was given her pick of the following three names for her son: Mochius, Sossius, and that of the martyr, Hotzazat. "That won't do," Akaky's late mother thought. "Those names are . . . how shall I put it . . ." To please her, the godparents opened the calendar at another page and again three names came out: Strifilius, Dulius, and Varachasius.

"We're in a mess," the old woman said. "Who ever heard of such names? If it was something like Varadat or Varuch, I wouldn't object . . . but Strifilius and Varachasius . . ."

So they turned to yet another page and out came Pavsicachius and Vachtisius.

"Well, that's that," the mother said. "That settles it. He'll just have to be Akaky like his father."

So that's how Akaky Akakievich originated.

And when they christened the child it cried and twisted its features into a sour expression as though it had a foreboding that it would become a ninth-class clerk.

Well, that's how it all happened, and it has been reported here just to show that the child couldn't have been called anything but Akaky.

No one remembers who helped him get his appointment to the department or when he started working there. Directors and all sorts of chiefs came and went, but he was always to be found at the same place, in the same position, and in the same capacity, that of copying clerk. Until, after a while, people began to believe that he must have been born just as he was, shabby frock coat, bald patch, and all.

In the office, not the slightest respect was shown him. The porters didn't get up when he passed. In fact, they didn't even raise their eyes, as if nothing but an ordinary fly had passed through the reception room. His chiefs were cold and despotic with him. Some head clerks would just thrust a paper under his nose without even saying, "Copy this," or "Here's a nice interesting little job for you," or some such pleasant remark as is current in well-bred offices. And Akaky Akakievich would take the paper without glancing up to see who had put it under his nose or whether the person was entitled to do so. And right away he would set about copying it.

The young clerks laughed at him and played tricks on him to the limit of their clerkish wit. They made up stories about him and told them in front of him. They said that his seventy-year-old landlady beat him and asked him when the wedding would be. They scattered scraps of paper which they said was snow over his head. But with all this going on, Akaky Akakievich never said a word and even acted as though no one were there. It didn't even affect his work, and in spite of their loud badgering he made no mistakes in his copying. Only when they tormented him unbearably, when they jogged his elbow and prevented him from getting on with his work, would he say:

"Let me be. Why do you do this to me? . . ."

And his words and the way he said them sounded strange. There was something touching about them. Once a young man who was new to the office started to tease him, following the crowd. Suddenly he stopped as if awakened from a trance and, after that, he couldn't stand the others, whom at first he had deemed decent people. And for a long time to come, during his gayest moments, he would suddenly see in his mind's eye the little, balding clerk and he would hear the words, "Let me be. Why do you do this to me?" and within those words rang the phrase, "I am your brother." And the young man would cover his face with his hands. Later in life he often shuddered, musing about the wickedness of man toward man and all the cruelty and vulgarity which are concealed under refined manners. And this, he decided, was also true of men who were considered upright and honorable.

It would be hard to find a man who so lived for his job. It would not be enough to say that he worked conscientiously—he worked with love. There, in his copying, he found an interesting, pleasant world for himself, and his delight was reflected in his face. He had his favorites among the letters of the alphabet and, when he came to them, he would chuckle, wink, and help them along with his lips so that they could almost be read on his face as they were formed by his pen.

Had he been rewarded in proportion with his zeal, he would,

perhaps to his own surprise, have been promoted to fifth-class clerk. But all he got out of it was, as his witty colleagues put it, a pin for his buttonhole and hemorrhoids to sit on.

Still, it would be unfair to say that no attention had ever been paid him. One of the successive directors, a kindly man, who thought Akaky Akakievich should be rewarded for his long service, suggested that he be given something more interesting than ordinary copying. So he was asked to prepare an already drawn-up document for referral to another department. Actually, all he had to do was to give it a new heading and change some of the verbs from the first to the third person. But Akaky Akakievich found this work so complicated that he broke into a sweat and finally, mopping his brow, he said:

"Oh no, I would rather have something to copy instead."

After that they left him to his copying forever. And aside from it, it seemed, nothing existed for him.

He never gave a thought to his clothes. His frock coat, which was supposed to be green, had turned a sort of mealy reddish. Its collar was very low and very narrow so that his neck, which was really quite ordinary, looked incredibly long—like the spring necks of the head-shaking plaster kittens which foreign peddlers carry around on their heads on trays. And, somehow, there was always something stuck to Akaky Akakievich's frock coat, a wisp of hay, a little thread. Then too, he had a knack of passing under windows just when refuse happened to be thrown out and as a result was forever carrying around on his hat melon rinds and other such rubbish.

Never did he pay any attention to what was going on around him in the street. In this he was very different from the other members of the pen-pushing brotherhood, who are so keen-eyed and observant that they'll notice an undone strap on the bottom of someone's trousers, an observation that unfailingly molds their features into a sly sneer. But even when Akaky

Akakievich's eyes were resting on something, he saw superimposed on it his own well-formed, neat handwriting. Perhaps it was only when, out of nowhere, a horse rested its head on his shoulder and sent a blast of wind down his cheek that he'd realize he was not in the middle of a line but in the middle of a street.

When he got home he would sit straight down to the table and quickly gulp his cabbage soup, followed by beef and onions. He never noticed the taste and ate it with flies and whatever else God happened to send along. When his stomach began to feel bloated, he would get up from the table, take out his inkwell, and copy papers he had brought with him from the office. And if there weren't any papers to copy for the office, he would make a copy for his own pleasure, especially if the document were unusual. Unusual, not for the beauty of its style, but because it was addressed to some new or important personage.

Even during those hours when light has completely disappeared from the gray Petersburg sky and the pen-pushing brotherhood have filled themselves with dinner of one sort or another, each as best he can according to his income and his preference; when everyone has rested from the scraping of pens in the office, from running around on their own and others' errands; when the restless human being has relaxed after the tasks, sometimes unnecessary, he sets himself; and the clerks hasten to give over the remaining hours to pleasure—the more enterprising among them rushes to the theater, another walks in the streets, allotting his time to the inspection of ladies' hats; another spends his evening paying compliments to some prettyish damsel, the queen of a small circle of clerks; another, the most frequent case, goes to visit a brother clerk, who lives somewhere on the third or fourth floor, in two small rooms with a hall of a kitchen and some little pretensions to fashion, a lamp or some other article bought at great sacrifice, such as going without dinner or outside pleasures—in brief, at the time when all clerks have dispersed among the lodgings of their friends to play a little game of whist, sipping tea from glasses and nibbling biscuits, inhaling the smoke from their long pipes, relaying, while the cards are dealt, some bit of gossip that has trickled down from high society, a thing which a Russian cannot do without whatever his circumstances, and even, when there's nothing else to talk about, telling once again the ancient joke about the commandant to whom it was reported that someone had hacked the tail off the horse of the monument to Peter the First—in a word, when everyone else was trying to have a good time, Akaky Akakievich was not even thinking of diverting himself.

No one had ever seen him at a party in the evening. Having written to his heart's content, he would go to bed, smiling in anticipation of the morrow, of what God would send him to copy.

Thus flowed the life of a man who, on a yearly salary of four hundred rubles, was content with his lot. And perhaps it would have flowed on to old age if it hadn't been for the various disasters which are scattered along life's paths, not only for ninth-class clerks, but even for eighth-, seventh-, sixth-class clerks and all the way up to State Councilors, Privy Councilors, and even to those who counsel no one, not even themselves.

In Petersburg, there's a formidable enemy for all those who receive a salary in the neighborhood of four hundred rubles a year. The enemy is none other than our northern cold, although they say it's very healthy.

Between eight and nine in the morning, at just the time when the streets are filled with people walking to their offices, the cold starts to mete out indiscriminately such hard, stinging flicks on noses that the wretched clerks don't know where to put them. And when the cold pinches the brows and brings tears to the eyes of those in high positions, ninth-class clerks are completely defenseless. They can only wrap themselves in their threadbare overcoats and run as fast as they can the five or six blocks to the office. Once arrived, they have to stamp their feet in the vestibule until their abilities and talents, which have been frozen on the way, thaw out once again.

Akaky Akakievich had noticed that for some time the cold had been attacking his back and shoulders quite viciously, try as he might to sprint the prescribed distance. He finally began to wonder whether the fault did not lie with his overcoat. When he gave it a good looking-over in his room, he discovered that in two or three places—the shoulders and back—it had become very much like gauze. The cloth was worn so thin that it let the draft in, and, to make things worse, the lining had disintegrated.

It must be noted that Akaky Akakievich's overcoat had also been a butt of the clerks' jokes. They had even deprived it of its respectable name, referring to it as the old dressing gown. And, as far as that goes, it did have a strange shape. Its collar shrank with every year, since it was used to patch other areas. And the patching, which did not flatter the tailor, made the overcoat baggy and ugly.

Having located the trouble, Akaky Akakievich decided to take the cloak to Petrovich, a tailor who lived somewhere on the fourth floor, up a back stairs, and who, one-eyed and pockmarked as he was, was still quite good at repairing clerks' and other such people's trousers and frock coats, provided he happened to be sober and hadn't other things on his mind.

We shouldn't, of course, waste too many words on the tailor, but since it has become the fashion to give a thorough description of every character figuring in a story, there's nothing to be done but to give you Petrovich.

At first he was called just Grigory and was the serf of some gentleman or other. He began to call himself Petrovich when he received his freedom and took to drinking rather heavily on all holidays, on the big ones at first and then, without distinction, on all church holidays—on any day marked by a little cross on the calendar. In this he was true to the traditions of his forefathers, and when his wife nagged him about it, he called her impious and a German. Now that we've mentioned his wife, we'd better say a word or two about her, too. But unfortunately very little is known about her, except that Petrovich had a wife who wore a bonnet instead of a kerchief but was apparently no beauty, since, on meeting her, it occurred to no one but an occasional soldier to peek under that bonnet of hers, twitching his mustache and making gurgling sounds.

Going up the stairs leading to Petrovich's place, which, to be honest about it, were saturated with water and slops and exuded that ammonia smell which burns your eyes and which you'll always find on the back stairs of all Petersburg houses—going up those stairs, Akaky Akakievich was already conjecturing how much Petrovich would ask and making up his mind not to pay more than two rubles.

The door stood open because Petrovich's wife was cooking some fish or other and had made so much smoke in the kitchen that you couldn't even see the cockroaches. Akaky Akakievich went through the kitchen without even seeing Mrs. Petrovich and finally reached the other room, where he saw Petrovich sitting on a wide, unpainted wooden table, with his legs crossed under him like a Turkish pasha.

He was barefoot, as tailors at work usually are, and the first thing Akaky Akakievich saw was Petrovich's big toe, with its twisted nail thick and hard like a tortoiseshell. A skein of silk and cotton thread hung around Petrovich's neck. On his knees there was some old garment. For the past three minutes he had been trying to thread his needle, very irritated at the darkness of the room and even with the thread itself, muttering under his breath, "It won't go through, the pig, it's killing me, the bitch!" Akaky Akakievich was unhappy to find Petrovich so irritated. He preferred to negotiate when the tailor was a little under the weather, or, as his wife put it, "when the one-eyed buzzard had a load on." When caught in such a state, Petrovich usually gave way very readily on the price and would even thank Akaky Akakievich with respectful bows and all that. True, afterwards his wife would come whining that her husband had charged too little because he was drunk; but all you had to do was to add ten kopeks and it was a deal.

This time, however, Petrovich seemed to be sober and therefore curt, intractable, and likely to charge an outrageous price. Akaky Akakievich realized this and would have liked to beat a hasty retreat, but the die was cast. Petrovich had fixed his one eye on him, and Akaky Akakievich involuntarily came out with:

"Hello, Petrovich."

"Wish you good day, sir," said Petrovich and bent his eye toward Akaky Akakievich's hands to see what kind of spoil he had brought him.

"Well, Petrovich, I've come . . . see . . . the thing is . . . to . . ."

It should be realized that Akaky Akakievich used all sorts of prepositions, adverbs, and all those meaningless little parts of speech when he spoke. Moreover, if the matter were very involved, he generally didn't finish his sentences and opened them with the words: "This, really, is absolutely, I mean to say . . ." and then nothing more—he had forgotten that he hadn't said what he wanted to.

"What is it then?" Petrovich asked, looking over Akaky Akakievich's frock coat with his one eye; the collar, the sleeves, the back, the tails, the buttonholes, all of which he was already acquainted with, since, repairs and all, it was his own work. That's just what tailors do as soon as they see you.

"Well, it's like this, Petrovich . . . my cloak, well, the material . . . look, you can see, everywhere else it's very strong, well, it's a bit dusty and it looks rather shabby, but it's not really . . . look, it's just in one place it's a little . . . on the back here, and here too . . . it's a little worn . . . and here on this shoulder too, a little—and that's all. There's not much work . . ."

Petrovich took Akaky Akakievich's old dressing gown, as his colleagues called it, spread it out on the table and looked it over at length. Then he shook his head and, stretching out his hand, took from the windowsill a snuffbox embellished with the portrait of a general, though just what general it was impossible to tell since right where his face used to be there was now a dent glued over with a piece of paper. Taking some snuff, Petrovich spread the overcoat out on his hands, held it up against the light, and again shook his head. Then he turned the overcoat inside out, with the lining up, and shook his head again. Then, once more, he removed the snuffbox lid with its general under the piece of paper, and, stuffing snuff into his nose, closed the box, put it away, and finally said:

"No. It can't be mended. It's no use."

At these words, Akaky Akakievich's heart turned over.

"But why can't it be, Petrovich?" he said in the imploring voice of a child. "Look, the only trouble is that it's worn around the shoulders. I'm sure you have some scraps of cloth . . ."

"As for scraps, I suppose I could find them," Petrovich said, "but I couldn't sew them on. The whole thing is rotten. It'd go to pieces the moment you touched it with a needle."

"Well, if it starts to go, you'll catch it with a patch . . ."

"But there's nothing for patches to hold to. It's too far gone. It's only cloth in name—a puff of wind and it'll disintegrate."

"Still, I'm sure you can make them hold just the same. Otherwise, really, Petrovich, see what I mean . . ."

"No," Petrovich said with finality, "nothing can be done with it. It's just no good. You'd better make yourself some bands out of it to wrap round your legs when it's cold and socks aren't enough to keep you warm. The Germans thought up those things to make money for themselves." (Petrovich liked to take a dig at the Germans whenever there was a chance.) "As to the overcoat, it looks as if you'll have to have a new one made."

At the word "new" Akaky Akakievich's vision became foggy and the whole room began to sway. The only thing he saw clearly was the general with the paper-covered face on the lid of Petrovich's snuffbox.

"What do you mean a *new* one?" he said, talking as if in a dream. "I haven't even got the money . . ."

"A new one," Petrovich repeated with savage calm.

"Well, but if I really had to have a new one, how would it be that . . ."

"That is, what will it cost?"

"Yes."

"Well, it will be over one hundred and fifty rubles," Petrovich said, pursing his lips meaningfully. He liked strong effects; he liked to perplex someone suddenly and then observe the grimace that his words produced.

"A hundred and fifty rubles for an overcoat!" shrieked the poor Akaky Akakievich, shrieked perhaps for the first time in his life, since he was always noted for his quietness.

"Yes, sir," said Petrovich, "but what an overcoat! And if it is to have marten on the collar and a silk-lined hood, that'll bring it up to two hundred."

"Please, Petrovich, please," Akaky Akakievich said beseechingly, not taking in Petrovich's words or noticing his dramatic effects, "mend it somehow, just enough to make it last a little longer."

"No sir, it won't work. It would be a waste of labor and money."

Akaky Akakievich left completely crushed. And when he left, Petrovich, instead of going back to his work, remained for a long time immobile, his lips pursed meaningfully. He was pleased with himself for having upheld his own honor as well as that of the entire tailoring profession.

Akaky Akakievich emerged into the street feeling as if he were in a dream. "So that's it," he repeated to himself. "I never suspected it would turn out this way . . ." And then, after a brief pause, he went on: "So that's it! Here's how it turns out in the end, and I, really, simply couldn't have foreseen it." After another, longer pause he added: "And so here we are! Here's how things stand. I in no way expected . . . but this is impossible . . . what a business!" Muttering thus, instead of going home, he went in the opposite direction, without having the slightest idea of what was going on.

As he was walking, a chimney sweep brushed his dirty side against him and blackened his whole shoulder; a whole bucketful of lime was showered over him from the top of a house under construction. But he noticed nothing, and only when he bumped into a watchman who, resting his halberd near him, was shaking some snuff out of a horn into his calloused palm, did he come to a little, and that only because the watchman said:

"Ya hafta knock my head off? Ya got the whole sidewalk, ain'tcha?"

This caused him to look about him and turn back toward home. Only then did he start to collect his thoughts and to see his real position clearly. He began to talk to himself, not in bits of phrases now but sensibly, as to a wise friend in whom he could confide.

"Oh no," he said, "this wasn't the moment to speak to Petrovich. Right now he's sort of . . . his wife obviously has given him a beating . . . that sort of thing. It'd be better if I went and saw him Sunday morning. After Saturday night, his one eye will be wandering and he'll be tired and in need of another drink, and his wife won't give him the money. So I'll slip him a quarter and that will make him more reasonable and so, for the overcoat . . ." Thus Akaky Akakievich tried to reassure himself, and persuaded himself to wait for Sunday.

When that day came, he waited at a distance until he saw Petrovich's wife leave the house and then went up. After his Saturday night libations, Petrovich's eye certainly was wandering. He hung his head and looked terribly sleepy. But, despite all that, as soon as he learned what Akaky Akakievich had come about, it was as if the devil had poked him.

"It can't be done," he said. "You must order a new one."

Here Akaky Akakievich pressed the quarter on him.

"Thank you," Petrovich said. "I'll drink a short one to you, sir. And as to the overcoat, you can stop worrying. It's worthless. But I'll make you a first-rate new one. That I'll see to."

Akaky Akakievich tried once more to bring the conversation around to mending, but Petrovich, instead of listening, said:

"I'll make you a new one, sir, and you can count on me to do my best. I may even make the collar fastened with silver-plated clasps for you."

At this point Akaky Akakievich saw that he'd have to have a new overcoat, and he became utterly depressed. Where was he going to get the money? There was of course the next holiday bonus. But the sum involved had long ago been allotted to other needs. He had to order new trousers, to pay the cobbler for replacing the tops on his boots. He owed the seamstress for three shirts and simply had to have two items of underwear which one cannot refer to in print. In fact, all the money, to the last kopek, was owed, and even if the director made an unexpectedly generous gesture and allotted him, instead of forty rubles, a whole forty-five or even fifty, the difference would be a drop in the ocean in the overcoat outlay.

It is true Akaky Akakievich knew that, on occasion, Petrovich slapped on heaven-knows-what exorbitant price, so that even his wife couldn't refrain from exclaiming:

"Have you gone mad, you fool! One day he accepts work for nothing, and the next, something gets into him and makes him ask for more than he's worth himself."

But he also knew that Petrovich would agree to make him a new overcoat for eighty rubles. Even so, where was he to find the eighty? He could perhaps scrape together half that sum. Even a little more. But where would he get the other half? . . . Let us, however, start with the first half and see where it was to come from.

Akaky Akakievich had a rule: whenever he spent one ruble, he slipped a copper into a little box with a slot in its side. Every six months, he counted the coppers and changed them for silver. He'd been doing this for a long time and, after all these years, had accumulated more than forty rubles. So this came to one half. But what about the remaining forty rubles?

Akaky Akakievich thought and thought and decided that he would have to reduce his regular expenses for an entire year at least. It would mean going without his evening tea, not burning candles at night, and, if he absolutely had to have light, going to his landlady's room and working by her candle. It would mean, when walking in the street, stepping as carefully as possible over the cobbles and paving stones, almost tiptoeing, so as not to wear out the soles of his boots too rapidly, and giving out his laundry as seldom as possible, and, so that it shouldn't get too soiled, undressing as soon as he got home and staying in just his thin cotton dressing gown, which, if time hadn't taken pity on it, would itself have collapsed long ago.

It must be admitted that, at first, he suffered somewhat from these restrictions. But then he became accustomed to them somehow, and things went smoothly again. He even got used to going hungry in the evenings, but then he was able to feed himself spiritually, carrying within him the eternal idea of his overcoat-to-be. It was as if his existence had become somehow fuller, as if he had married and another human being were there with him, as if he were no longer alone on life's road but walking by the side of a delightful companion. And that companion was none other than the overcoat itself, with its thick padding and strong lining that would last forever. In some way, he became more alive, even stronger-minded, like a man who has determined his ultimate goal in life.

From his face and actions all the marks of vacillation and indecision vanished.

At times there was even a fire in his eyes, and the boldest, wildest notions flashed through his head—perhaps he should really consider having marten put on the collar? The intensity of these thoughts almost distracted his attention from his work. Once he almost made a mistake, which caused him to exclaim—true, very softly—"Oof!" and to cross himself.

At least once each month he looked in on Petrovich to discuss the overcoat—the best place to buy the material, its color, its price . . . Then, on the way home, a little worried but always pleased, he mused about how, finally, all this buying would be over and the coat would be made.

Things went ahead faster than he had expected. Beyond all expectations, the director granted Akaky Akakievich not forty, nor forty-five, but a whole sixty rubles. Could he have had a premonition that Akaky Akakievich needed a new overcoat, or had it just happened by itself? Whatever it was, Akaky Akakievich wound up with an extra twenty rubles. This circumstance speeded matters up. Another two or three months of moderate hunger and he had almost all of the eighty rubles he needed. His heartbeat, generally very quiet, grew faster.

As soon as he could, he set out for the store with Petrovich. They bought excellent material, which is not surprising since they had been planning the move for all of six months, and a month had seldom gone by without Akaky Akakievich dropping into the shop to work out prices. Petrovich himself said that there was no better material to be had.

For the lining they chose calico, but so good and thick that, Petrovich said, it even looked better and glossier than silk. They did not buy marten because it was too expensive. Instead they got cat, the best available—cat which at a distance could always be taken for marten. Petrovich spent two full weeks on the overcoat because of all the quilting he had to do. He charged twelve rubles for his work—it was impossible to take less: it had been sewn with silk, with fine double seams, and Petrovich had gone over each seam again afterwards with his own teeth, squeezing out different patterns with them.

It was—well, it's hard to say exactly which day it was, but it was probably the most solemn day in Akaky Akakievich's life, the day Petrovich finally brought him the overcoat. He brought it in the morning, just before it was time to go to the office. There couldn't have been a better moment for the coat to arrive, because cold spells had been creeping in and threatened to become even more severe. Petrovich appeared with the coat, as befits a good tailor. He had an expression of importance on his face that Akaky Akakievich had never seen before. He looked very much aware of having performed an important act, an act that carried tailors over the chasm which separates those who merely put in linings and do repairs from those who create.

He took the overcoat out of the gigantic handkerchief—just fresh from the wash—in which he had wrapped it to deliver it. The handkerchief he folded neatly and put in his pocket, ready for use. Then he took the coat, looked at it with great pride and, holding it in both hands, threw it quite deftly around Akaky Akakievich's shoulders. He pulled and smoothed it down at the back, wrapped it around Akaky Akakievich, leaving it a little open at the front. Akaky Akakievich, a down-to-earth sort of man, wanted to try out the sleeves. Petrovich helped him to pull his arms through, and it turned out that with the sleeves, too, it was good. In a word, it was clear that the coat fitted perfectly.

Petrovich didn't fail to take advantage of the occasion to remark that it was only because he did without a signboard, lived in a small side street, and had known Akaky Akakievich for a long time that he had charged him so little. On Nevsky Avenue, nowadays, he said, they'd have taken seventy-five rubles for the work alone. Akaky Akakievich had no desire to debate the point with Petrovich—he was always rather awed by the big sums which Petrovich liked to mention to impress people. He paid up, thanked Petrovich, and left for the office wearing his new overcoat.

Petrovich followed him and stood for a long time in the street, gazing at the overcoat from a distance. Then he plunged into a curving side street, took a short cut, and reemerged on the street ahead of Akaky Akakievich, so that he could have another look at the coat from another angle.

Meanwhile, Akaky Akakievich walked on, bubbling with good spirits. Every second of every minute he felt the new overcoat on his shoulders, and several times he even let out a little chuckle of inward pleasure. Indeed, the overcoat presented him with a double advantage: it was warm and it was good. He didn't notice his trip at all and suddenly found himself before the office building. In the porter's lodge, he slipped off the overcoat, inspected it, and entrusted it to the porter's special care.

No one knows how, but it suddenly became general knowledge in the office that Akaky Akakievich had a new overcoat and that the old dressing gown no longer existed. Elbowing one another, they all rushed to the cloakroom to see the new coat. Then they proceeded to congratulate him. He smiled at first, but then the congratulations became too exuberant and he felt embarrassed. And when they surrounded him and started trying to persuade him that the very least he could do was to invite them over one evening to drink to the coat, Akaky Akakievich felt completely at a loss, didn't know what to do with himself, what to say or how to talk himself out of it. And a few minutes later, all red in the face, he was trying rather naively to convince them that it wasn't a new overcoat at all, that it wasn't much, that it was an old one.

In the end, a clerk, no lesser person than an assistant to the head clerk, probably wanting to show that he wasn't too proud to mingle with those beneath him, said:

"All right then, I'll do it instead of Akaky Akakievich. I invite you all over for a party. Come over to my place tonight. Incidentally, it happens to be my birthday today."

Naturally the clerks now congratulated the head clerk's assistant and happily accepted his invitation. Akaky Akakievich started to excuse himself, but he was told that it would be rude on his part, a disgrace, so he had to give way in the end. And later he was even rather pleased that he had accepted, since it would give him an opportunity to wear the new coat in the evening too.

Akaky Akakievich felt as if it were a holiday. He arrived home in the happiest frame of mind, took off the overcoat, hung it up very carefully on the wall, gave the material and the lining one more admiring inspection. Then he took out that ragged item known as the old dressing gown and put it next to the new overcoat, looked at it, and began to laugh, so great was the difference between the two. And long after that, while eating his dinner, he snorted every time he thought of the dressing gown. He felt very gay during his dinner, and afterwards he did no copying whatsoever. Instead he wallowed in luxury for a while, lying on his bed until dark. Then, without further dallying, he dressed, pulled on his new overcoat, and went out.

It is, alas, impossible to say just where the party-giving clerk lived. My memory is beginning to fail me badly and everything in Petersburg, streets and houses, has become so mixed up in my head that it's very difficult to extract anything from it and to present it in an orderly fashion. Be that as it may, it is a fact that the clerk in question lived in a better district of the city, which means not too close to Akaky Akakievich.

To start with, Akaky Akakievich had to pass through a maze of deserted, dimly lit streets, but, toward the clerk's house, the streets became lighter and livelier. More pedestrians began flashing by more often; there were some well-dressed ladies and men with beaver collars. And, instead of the drivers with their wooden, fretworked sledges studded with gilt nails, he came across smart coachmen in crimson velvet caps, in lacquered sledges, with bearskin lap rugs. He even saw some carriages darting past with decorated boxes, their wheels squeaking on the snow.

Akaky Akakievich gazed around him. For several years now he hadn't been out in the evening. He stopped before the small, lighted window of a shop, staring curiously at a picture of a pretty woman kicking off her shoe and thereby showing her whole leg, which was not bad at all; in the background, some man or other with side whiskers and a handsome Spanish goatee was sticking his head through a door leading to another room. Akaky Akakievich shook his head, snorted, smiled, and walked on. Why did he snort? Was it because he had come across something that, although completely strange to him, still aroused in him, as it would in anyone, a certain instinct—or did he think, as many clerks do, along the following lines: "Well, really, the French! If they are after something . . . that sort of thing . . . then, really! . . ." Maybe he didn't even think that. After all, one can't just creep into a man's soul and find out everything he's thinking.

At last he reached the house in which the head clerk's assistant lived. And he lived in style, on the second floor, with the staircase lighted by a lantern. In the hall, Akaky Akakievich found several rows of galoshes. Amidst the galoshes, a samovar was hissing and puffing steam. All around the walls hung overcoats and cloaks, some with beaver collars and others with velvet lapels. The noise and talk that could be heard through the partition became suddenly clear and resounding when the door opened and a servant came out with a tray of empty glasses, a cream jug, and a basket of cookies. It was clear that the clerks had arrived long before and had already drunk their first round of tea.

Akaky Akakievich hung his coat up and went in. In a flash, he took in the candles, the clerks, the pipes, the card tables, while his ears were filled with the hubbub of voices rising all around him and the banging of chairs being moved. Awkwardly, he paused in the middle of the room, trying to think what to do. But he had been noticed, and his arrival was greeted with a huge yell. Immediately everybody rushed out into the hall to have another look at his new overcoat. Akaky Akakievich felt a bit confused, but, being an uncomplicated man, he was rather pleased when everyone agreed that it was a good overcoat.

Soon, however, they abandoned him and his overcoat and turned their attention, as was to be expected, to the card tables.

The din, the voices, the presence of so many people—all this was unreal to Akaky Akakievich. He had no idea how to behave, where to put his hands, his feet, or, for that matter, his whole body. He sat down near a card table, stared at the cards, and peeked in turn into the faces of the players. In a little while he got bored and began to yawn, feeling rather sleepy—it was long past his usual bedtime. He wanted to take leave of the host, but they wouldn't let him go. He really had to toast his new overcoat with champagne, they insisted. They made Akaky Akakievich drink two glasses of champagne, after which he felt that the party was becoming gayer, but nevertheless he was quite unable to forget that it was now midnight and that he should have gone home long ago.

In spite of everything his host could think up to keep him, he went quietly out into the hall, found his overcoat, which to his annoyance was lying on the floor, shook it, carefully removed every speck he could find on it, put it on, and walked down the stairs and out into the street.

The street was still lighted. Some little stores, those meeting places for servants and people of every sort, were open, while others, although closed, still showed a long streak of light under their doors, which indicated that the company had not yet dispersed and that the menservants and maids were finishing up their gossip and their conversations, leaving their masters perplexed as to their whereabouts.

Akaky Akakievich walked along in such a gay mood that, who knows why, he almost darted after a lady who flashed by him like a streak of lightning, every part of her body astir with independent, fascinating motion. Still, he restrained himself immediately, went back to walking slowly and even wondered where that compulsion to gallop had come from.

Soon there stretched out before him those deserted streets which, even in the daytime, are not so gay, and, now that it was night, looked even more desolate. Fewer street lamps were lit—obviously a smaller oil allowance was given out in this district. Then came wooden houses and fences; not a soul around, nothing but glistening snow and the black silhouettes of the low, sleeping hovels with their shuttered windows. He came to the spot where the street cut through a square so immense that the houses opposite were hardly visible beyond its sinister emptiness.

God knows where, far away on the edge of the world, he could see the glow of a brazier by a watchman's hut.

Akaky Akakievich's gay mood definitely waned. He could not suppress a shiver as he stepped out into the square, a foreboding of evil in his heart. He glanced behind him and to either side—it was like being in the middle of the sea. "No, it's better not to look," he thought, and walked on with his eyes shut. And when he opened them again to see if the other side of the square was close, he saw instead, standing there, almost in front of his nose, people with mustaches, although he couldn't make out exactly who or what. Then his vision became foggy and there was a beating in his chest.

"Why, here's my overcoat," one of the people thundered, grabbing him by the collar.

Akaky Akakievich was just going to shout out, "Help!" when another brought a fist about the size of a clerk's head up to his very mouth, and said:

"You just try and yell . . ."

Akaky Akakievich felt them pull off his coat, then he received a knee in the groin. He went down on his back, and after that he lay in the snow and felt nothing more.

When he came to a few minutes later and scrambled to his feet, there was no one around. He felt cold and, when he realized that the overcoat was gone, desperate. He let out a yell. But his voice didn't come close to reaching the other side of the square.

Frantic, he hollered all the way across the square as he scrambled straight toward the watchman's hut. The watchman was standing beside it, leaning on his halberd, and gazing out across the square, wondering who it could be running toward him and shouting. At last Akaky Akakievich reached him. Gasping for breath, he began shouting at him—what sort of a watchman did he think he was, hadn't he seen anything, and why the devil had he allowed them to rob a man? The watchman said he had seen no one except the two men who had stopped Akaky Akakievich in the middle of the square, who he had thought were friends of his, and that instead of hollering at the watchman, he'd better go and see the police inspector tomorrow and the inspector would find out who had taken the overcoat.

Akaky Akakievich hurried home; he was in a terrible state. The little hair he had left, on his temples and on the back of his head, was completely disheveled; there was snow all down one side of him and on his chest and all over his trousers. His old landlady, hearing his impatient banging on the door, jumped out of bed and, with only one shoe on, ran to open up, clutching her nightgown at the neck, probably out of modesty. When she saw the state Akaky Akakievich was in, she stepped back.

When he told her what had happened, she threw up her hands and said that he should go straight to the borough Police Commissioner, that the local police inspector could not be trusted, that he'd just make promises and give him the runaround. So it was best, she said, to go straight to the borough Commissioner. In fact, she even knew him because Anna, her former Finnish cook, had now got a job as a nanny at his house. And the landlady herself often saw him driving past their house. Moreover, she knew he went to church every Sunday and prayed and at the same time looked cheerful and was obviously a good man. Having heard her advice, Akaky Akakievich trudged off sadly to his room and somehow got through the night, though exactly how must be imagined by those who know how to put themselves in another man's place.

Early the next morning, he went to the borough Commissioner's. But it turned out that he was still asleep. He returned at ten and again was told that he was asleep. He went back at eleven and was told that the Commissioner was not home. He tried again during the dinner hour, but the secretaries in the reception room would not let him in and wanted to know what business had brought him. For once in his life Akaky Akakievich decided to show some character and told them curtly that he must see the Commissioner personally, that they'd better let him in since he was on official government business, that he would lodge a complaint against them, and that then they would see.

The secretaries didn't dare say anything to that, and one of them went to call the Commissioner. The Commissioner reacted very strangely to Akaky Akakievich's story of the robbery. Instead of concentrating on the main point, he asked Akaky Akakievich what he had been doing out so late, whether he had stopped off somewhere on his way, hadn't he been to a house of ill repute. Akaky Akakievich became very confused, and when he left he wasn't sure whether something would be done about his overcoat or not.

That day he did not go to his office for the first time in his life. The next day he appeared, looking very pale and wearing his old dressing gown, which now seemed shabbier than ever. His account of the theft of his overcoat touched many of the clerks, although, even now, there were some who poked fun at him. They decided on the spot to take up a collection for him, but they collected next to nothing because the department employees had already had to donate money for a portrait of the Director and to subscribe to some book or other, on the suggestion of the section chief, who was a friend of the author's. So the sum turned out to be the merest trifle.

Someone, moved by compassion, decided to help Akaky Akakievich by giving him good advice. He told him that he had better not go to his local inspector because, even supposing the inspector wanted to impress his superiors and managed to recover the coat, Akaky Akakievich would still find it difficult to obtain it at the police station unless he could present irrefutable proof of ownership. The best thing was to go through a certain important personage who, by writing and contacting the right people, would set things moving faster. So Akaky Akakievich decided to seek an audience with the important personage.

Even to this day, it is not known exactly what position the important personage held or what his duties consisted of. All we need to know is that this important personage had become important quite recently and that formerly he had been an unimportant person. And even his present position was unimportant compared with other, more important ones. But there is always a category of people for whom somebody who is unimportant to others is an important personage. And the personage in question used various devices to play up his importance: for instance, he made the civil servants of lower categories come out to meet him on the stairs before he'd even reached his office; and a subordinate could not approach him directly but had to go through proper channels. That's the way things are in Holy Russia—everyone tries to ape his superior.

They say that one ninth-class clerk, when he was named

section chief in a small office, immediately had a partition put up to make a separate room, which he called the conference room. He stationed an usher at the door who had to open it for all those who came in, although the conference room had hardly enough space for a writing table, even without visitors. The audiences and the manner of our important personage were impressive and stately, but quite uncomplicated. The key to his system was severity. He liked to say "Severity, severity, severity," and as he uttered the word for the third time, he usually looked very meaningfully into the face of the person he was talking to. True, it was not too clear what need there was for all this severity since the ten-odd employees who made up the whole administrative apparatus of his office were quite frightened enough as it was. Seeing him coming, they would leave their work and stand to attention until he had crossed the room. His usual communication with his inferiors was full of severity and consisted almost entirely of three phrases: "How dare you!" "Who do you think you're talking to?" and "Do you appreciate who I am?" Actually, he was a kindly man, a good friend and obliging, but promotion to a high rank had gone to his head, knocked him completely off balance, and he just didn't know how to act. When he happened to be with equals, he was still a decent fellow and, in a way, by no means stupid. But whenever he found himself among those who were below him—even a single rank—he became impossible. He fell silent and was quite pitiable, because even he himself realized that he could have been having a much better time. Sometimes he was obviously longing to join some group in a lively conversation, but he would be stopped by the thought that he would be going too far, putting himself on familiar terms and thereby losing face. And so he remained eternally in silent, aloof isolation, only occasionally uttering some monosyllabic sounds, and, as a result, he acquired a reputation as a deadly bore.

It was to this important personage that Akaky Akakievich presented himself, and at a most unpropitious moment to boot. That is, very unpropitious for him, although quite suitable for the important personage. The latter was in his office talking gaily to a childhood friend who had recently come to Petersburg and whom he hadn't seen for many years. This was the moment when they announced that there was a man named Shoenik to see him.

"Who's he?" the personage wanted to know.

"Some clerk," they told him.

"I see. Let him wait. I am not available now."

Here it should be noted that the important personage was greatly exaggerating. He was available. He and his friend had talked over everything imaginable. For some time now the conversation had been interlaced with lengthy silences, and they weren't doing much more than slapping each other on the thigh and saying:

"So that's how it is, Ivan Abramovich."

"Yes, indeed, Stepan Varlamovich!"

Still Akaky Akakievich had to wait, so that his friend, who had left the government service long ago and now lived in the country, could see what a long time employees had to wait in his reception room.

At last, when they had talked and had sat silent facing each other for as long as they could stand it, when they had smoked a cigar reclining in comfortable armchairs with sloping backs, the important personage, as if he had just recalled it, said to his secretary who was standing at the door with papers for a report:

"Wait a minute. Wasn't there a clerk waiting? Tell him to come in."

Seeing Akaky Akakievich's humble appearance and his wretched old frock coat, he turned abruptly to face him and said: "What do you want?"

He spoke in the hard, sharp voice which he had deliberately developed by practicing at home before a mirror an entire week before he had taken over his present exalted position.

Akaky Akakievich, who had felt properly subdued even before this, felt decidedly embarrassed. He did his best, as far as he could control his tongue, to explain what had happened. Of course, he added even more than his usual share of phrases like "that is to say" and "so to speak." The overcoat, he explained, was completely new and had been cruelly taken away from him, and he had turned to the important personage, that is to say, come to him, in the hope that he would, so to speak, intercede for him somehow, that is to say, write to the Superintendent of Police or, so to speak, to someone, and find the overcoat.

For some unimaginable reason the important personage found his manner too familiar.

"My dear sir," he answered sharply, "don't you know the proper channels? Do you realize whom you're addressing and what the proper procedure should be? You should first have handed in a petition to the office. It would have gone to the head clerk. From him it would have reached the section head, who would have approached my secretary, and only then would the secretary have presented it to me . . ."

"But, Your Excellency," said Akaky Akakievich, trying to gather what little composure he had and feeling at the same time that he was sweating terribly, "I, Your Excellency, ventured to trouble you because secretaries, that is to say . . . are, so to speak, an unreliable lot . . ."

"What, what, what?" demanded the important personage. "Where did you pick up such an attitude? Where did you get such ideas? What is this insubordination that is spreading among young people against their chiefs and superiors?"

The important personage, apparently, had not noticed that Akaky Akakievich was well over fifty. Thus, surely, if he could be called young at all it would only be relative, that is, to someone of seventy.

"Do you realize to whom you are talking? Do you appreciate who I am? Do you really realize, do you, I'm asking you?"

Here he stamped his foot and raised his voice to such a pitch that there was no need to be an Akaky Akakievich to be frightened.

And Akaky Akakievich froze completely. He staggered, his whole body shook, and he was quite unable to keep his feet. If a messenger hadn't rushed over and supported him, he would have collapsed onto the floor. They carried him out almost unconscious.

And the important personage, pleased to see that his dramatic effect had exceeded his expectations, and completely delighted with the idea that a word from him could knock a man unconscious, glanced at his friend to see what he thought of it all and was pleased to see that the friend looked somewhat at a loss and that fear had extended to him too.

Akaky Akakievich remembered nothing about getting downstairs and out into the street. He could feel neither hand nor foot. In all his life he had never been so severely reprimanded by a high official, and not a direct chief of his at that. He walked open-mouthed through a blizzard, again and again stumbling off the sidewalk. The wind, according to Petersburg custom, blew at him from all four sides at once, out of every side street. In no time it had blown him a sore throat, and he got himself home at last quite unable to say a word. His throat was swollen and he went straight to bed. That's how severe the effects of an adequate reprimand can be.

The next day he was found to have a high fever. Thanks to the generous assistance of the Petersburg climate, the illness progressed beyond all expectations. A doctor came, felt his pulse, found there was nothing he could do, and prescribed a poultice. That was done so that the patient would not be deprived of the beneficial aid of medicine. The doctor added, however, that, by the way, the patient had another day and a half to go, after which he would be what is called kaput. Then, turning to the landlady, the doctor said:

"And you, my good woman, I'd not waste my time if I were you. I'd order him the coffin right away. A pine one. The oak ones, I imagine, would be too expensive for him."

Whether Akaky Akakievich heard what for him were fateful words, and, if he heard, whether they had a shattering effect on him and whether he was sorry to lose his wretched life, are matters of conjecture. He was feverish and delirious the whole time. Apparitions, each stranger than the last, kept crowding before him. He saw Petrovich and ordered an overcoat containing some sort of concealed traps to catch the thieves who were hiding under his bed, so that every minute he kept calling his landlady to come and pull out the one who had even slipped under his blanket. Next, he would ask why his old dressing gown was hanging there in front of him when he had a new overcoat. Then he would find himself standing before the important personage, listening to the reprimand and repeating over and over: "I am sorry, Your Excellency, I am sorry."

Then he began to swear, using the most frightful words, which caused his old landlady to cross herself in horror; never in her life had she heard anything like it from him, and what made it even worse was that they came pouring out on the heels of the phrase, "Your Excellency." After that he talked complete nonsense, and it was impossible to make out anything he was saying, except that his disconnected words kept groping for that lost overcoat of his. Then, at last, poor Akaky Akakievich gave up the ghost.

They did not bother to seal his room or his belongings because there were no heirs and, moreover, very little to inherit—namely, a bundle of goose quills, a quire of white government paper, three pairs of socks, a few buttons that had come off his trousers, and the old dressing-gown coat already mentioned. God knows whom they went to; even the reporter of this story did not care enough to find out.

They took Akaky Akakievich away and buried him. And Petersburg went on without him exactly as if he had never existed. A creature had vanished, disappeared. He had had no one to protect him. No one had ever paid him the slightest attention. Not even that which a naturalist pays to a common fly which he mounts on a pin and looks at through his microscope. True, this creature, who had meekly borne the office jokes and gone quietly to his grave, had had, toward the end of his life, a cherished visitor—the overcoat, which for a brief moment had brightened his wretched existence. Then a crushing blow had finished everything, a blow such as befalls the powerful of the earth . . .

A few days after his death, a messenger from his office was sent to his lodgings with an order summoning him to report immediately; the chief was asking for him. But the messenger had to return alone and to report that Akaky Akakievich could not come.

"Why not?" he was asked.

"Because," the messenger said, "he died. They buried him four days ago."

That is how the department found out about Akaky Akakievich's death, and the next day a new clerk sat in his place: he was much taller and his handwriting was not as straight. In fact, his letters slanted considerably.

But who would have imagined that that was not the end of Akaky Akakievich, that he was fated to live on and make his presence felt for a few days after his death as if in compensation for having spent his life unnoticed by anyone? But that's the way it happened, and our little story gains an unexpectedly fantastic ending. Rumors suddenly started to fly around Petersburg that a ghost was haunting the streets at night in the vicinity of the Kalinkin Bridge. The ghost, which looked like a little clerk, was purportedly searching for a stolen overcoat and used this pretext to pull the coats off the shoulders of everyone he met without regard for rank or title. And it made no difference what kind of coat it was—cat, beaver, fox, bearskin, in fact any of the furs and skins people have thought up to cover their own skins with.

One of the department employees saw the ghost with his own eyes and instantly recognized Akaky Akakievich. However, he was so terrified that he dashed off as fast as his legs would carry him and so didn't get a good look; he only saw from a distance that the ghost was shaking his finger at him. Complaints kept pouring in, and not only from petty employees, which would have been understandable. One and all, even Privy Councilors, were catching chills in their backs and shoulders from having their overcoats peeled off. The police were ordered to catch the ghost at any cost, dead or alive, and to punish him with due severity as a warning to others. And what's more, they nearly succeeded.

To be precise, a watchman caught the ghost red-handed, grabbed it by the collar, in Kiryushkin Alley, as it was trying to pull the coat off a retired musician who, in his day, used to tootle on the flute. Grabbing it, he called for help from two colleagues of his and asked them to hold on to it for just a minute. He had, he said, to get his snuffbox out of his boot so that he could bring some feeling back to his nose, which had been frostbitten six times in his life. But it was evidently snuff that even a ghost couldn't stand. The man, closing his right nostril with his finger, had hardly sniffed up half a fistful into the left when the ghost sneezed so violently that the three watchmen were blinded by the resulting shower. They all raised their fists to wipe their eyes and, when they could see again, the ghost had vanished. They even wondered whether they had really held him at all. After that, watchmen were so afraid of the ghost that they felt reluctant to interfere with live robbers and contented themselves with shouting from a distance: "Hey you! On your way!"

And the clerk's ghost began to haunt the streets well beyond the Kalinkin Bridge, spreading terror among the meek.

However, we have completely neglected the important personage, who really, in a sense, was the cause of the fantastic direction that this story—which, by the way, is completely true—has taken. First of all, it is only fair to say that shortly after poor Akaky Akakievich, reduced to a pulp, had left his office, the important personage felt a twinge of regret. Compassion was not foreign to him—many good impulses stirred his heart, although his position usually prevented them from coming to the surface. As soon as his visiting friend had left the office, his thoughts returned to Akaky Akakievich. And after that, almost every day, he saw in his mind's eye the bloodless face of the little clerk who had been unable to take a proper reprimand. This thought was so disturbing that a week later he went so far as to send a clerk from his office to see how Akaky Akakievich was doing and to find out whether, in fact, there was any way to help him. And when he heard the news that Akaky Akakievich had died suddenly of a fever, it was almost a blow to him, even made him feel guilty and spoiled his mood for the whole day.

Trying to rid himself of these thoughts, to forget the whole unpleasant business, he went to a party at a friend's house. There he found himself in respectable company and, what's more, among people nearly all of whom were of the same standing so that there was absolutely nothing to oppress him. A great change came over him. He let himself go, chatted pleasantly, was amiable, in a word, spent a very pleasant evening. At supper, he drank a couple of glasses of champagne, a well-recommended prescription for inducing good spirits. The champagne gave him an inclination for something special, and so he decided not to go home but instead to pay a little visit to a certain well-known lady named Karolina Ivanovna, a lady, it seems, of German extraction, toward whom he felt very friendly. It should be said that the important personage was no longer a young man, that he was a good husband, the respected father of a family. His two sons, one of whom already had a civil-service post, and his sweet-faced sixteen-year-old daughter, who had a slightly hooked but nevertheless pretty little nose, greeted him every day with a "*Bonjour*, Papa." His wife, a youngish woman and not unattractive at that, gave him her hand to kiss and then kissed his. But although the important personage was quite content with these displays of family affection, he considered it the proper thing to do to have, for friendship's sake, a lady friend in another part of the city. This lady friend was not a bit prettier or younger than his wife, but the world is full of such puzzling things and it is not our business to judge them.

So the important personage came down the steps, stepped into his sledge, and said to the coachman:

"To Karolina Ivanovna's."

Wrapping his warm, luxurious fur coat around him, he sat back in his seat. He was in that state so cherished by Russians, in which without your having to make any effort, thoughts, each one pleasanter than the last, slip into your head by themselves.

Perfectly content, he went over all the most pleasant moments at the party, over the clever retorts that had caused that select gathering to laugh. He even repeated many of them under his breath and, still finding them funny, laughed heartily at them all over again, which was natural enough. However, he kept being bothered by gusts of wind which would suddenly blow, God knows from where or for what reason, cutting his face, throwing lumps of snow into it, filling the cape of his coat like a sail, and throwing it over his head, so that he had to extricate himself from it again and again.

Suddenly the important personage felt someone grab him violently from behind. He turned around and saw a small man in a worn-out frock coat. Terrified, he recognized Akaky Akakievich, his face as white as the snow and looking altogether very ghostly indeed. Fear took over completely when the important personage saw the ghost's mouth twist and, sending a whiff of the grave into his face, utter the following words:

"I've caught you at last. I've got you by the collar now! It's the coat I need. You did nothing about mine and hollered at me to boot. Now I'll take yours!"

The poor important personage almost died. He may have displayed force of character in the office and, in general, toward his inferiors, so that after one glance at his strong face and manly figure, people would say, "Quite a man," but now, like many other mighty-looking people, he was so frightened that he began to think, and not without reason, that he was about to have an attack of something or other. He was even very helpful in peeling off his coat, after which he shouted to the coachman in a ferocious tone:

"Home! As fast as you can!"

The coachman, hearing the ferocious tone which the important personage used in critical moments and which was sometimes accompanied with something even more drastic, instinctively ducked his head and cracked his whip, so that they tore away like a streak. In a little over six minutes the important personage was in front of his house. Instead of being at Karolina Ivanovna's, he was somehow staggering to his room, pale, terrified, and coatless. There he spent such a restless night that the next morning, at breakfast, his daughter said:

"You look terribly pale this morning, Papa."

But Papa was silent, and he didn't say a word to anyone about what had happened to him, or where he had been, or where he had intended to go. This incident made a deep impression upon him. From then on his subordinates heard far less often: "How dare you!" and "Do you know whom you're talking to?" And even when he did use these expressions, it was after listening to what others had to say.

But even more remarkable—after that night, Akaky Akakievich's ghost was never seen again. The important personage's overcoat must have fitted him snugly. At any rate, one no longer heard of coats being torn from people's shoulders. However, many busybodies wouldn't let the matter rest there and maintained that the ghost was still haunting certain distant parts of the city. And, sure enough, a watchman in the Kolomna district caught a glimpse of the ghost behind a house. But he was rather a frail watchman. (Once an ordinary, but mature, piglet, rushing out of a private house, knocked him off his feet to the huge delight of a bunch of cabbies, whom he fined two kopeks each for their lack of respect—then he spent the proceeds on tobacco.) So, being rather frail, the watchman didn't dare to arrest the ghost. Instead he followed it in the darkness until at last it stopped suddenly, turned to face him, and asked:

"You looking for trouble?"

And it shook a huge fist at him, much larger than any you'll find among the living.

"No," the watchman said, turning away.

This ghost, however, was a much taller one and wore an enormous mustache. It walked off, it seems, in the direction of the Obukhov Bridge and soon dissolved into the gloom of night.

Interpretive Questions

1. Why do Akaky's actions and feelings begin to change when he gets his new coat?

2. Why does a second ghost appear after Akaky's ghost was never seen again? Why does the second ghost have a huge fist and a mustache?

3. Would Akaky have been better off if he had not obtained the new overcoat?

4. Why does the loss of his new overcoat make Akaky decide for the first time in his life "to show some character"?

5. Why does Akaky love being a ninth-class clerk?